THE REBOOT

THE REBOOT

RECONNECTING FATHERS WITH THEIR SONS AND DAUGHTERS

BY WALTER L. RATCLIFFE

Copyright © 2024 Walter L. Ratcliffe
Editing by: Dirty Truth Publishing
A Truth Matters Press Book
All rights reserved.

All scripture taken from versions of the Holy Bible as indicated.

No part of this book may be reproduced or transmitted in any form whatsoever, electronic, or mechanical, including photocopying, recording, or by any informational storage or retrieval without the expressed written consent of the publisher, except in the brief quotation in critical articles or reviews.

Inquiries regarding permission for use of the material contained in this book should be addressed to:
Walter L. Ratcliffe, waltrat3@gmail.com.

ISBN: 9798218451974

First Edition.

Printed in the United States of America.

~ Dedication ~

This book is dedicated to my mother Rose Peebles Ratcliffe, to my father Walter L. Ratcliffe, to my wife April, my children: Cheryl, Ray, and Christian, and to everyone who has struggled with and survived the effects of fatherlessness in their lives.

~ Contents ~

Foreword 11

Introduction: Why Another Book on Fatherlessness? 13

Chapter 1. I Don't Have a Father 19

Chapter 2. How Come He Don't Want Me? 23

Chapter 3. What Happens When Fathers Aren't Around ... 31

Chapter 4. Like Father Like Son 39

Chapter 5. Heroes 49

Chapter 6. Heroes 'Rescue' Their Children 55

Chapter 7. Heroes 'Restore' Their Children 67

Chapter 8. What Every Son Needs From a Father 77

Chapter 9. Daddy's Little Girl 87

Chapter 10. He's Called to Be Father, Not Friend 97

Chapter 11. A Generation That Did Not Know God 105

Chapter 12. Real Talk 115

The Ten Commandments of Fatherhood 123

The Father Covenant 125

Absent Fathers by Rose P. Ratcliffe 126

Resources 128

About the Author 131

~ Foreword ~

The greatest teacher that ever lived was the One they called Master, Jesus Christ. Jesus would teach divine truth with such simplicity that even the most uneducated people could understand the things He would expound on.

Jesus was so skillful in using metaphors, earthly examples, and practical parables (stories) to reveal spiritual truths. Jesus used examples like a mustard seed, a fig tree, a vine, a branch, a pearl, a fisherman's net, and many other simple things to unveil great truths.

In the fashion of Jesus, I have attempted to use various teaching techniques like that of the Master to open hearts and minds to the importance of reconnecting fathers with their sons and daughters.

The illustrations, stories, and movie references are not to entertain, but to solely create a connection with you on this critical and urgent subject.

So please follow me on this journey of "rebooting" the relationships of fathers with their children.

And as with everything, may God get the glory out of this manuscript that I believe has been inspired by Him.

Sincerely,

Walter L. Ratcliffe

~ Introduction ~

Why another Book on Fatherlessness?

The critical nature of the phenomena of fatherlessness in this nation, the effect that it has had, and continues to have in the lives of children both young and old, and families, is why I believe that God put it on my heart to write this book. I am not a writer, nor a scholar, but simply one who has seen and experienced the effects of the absence of a father in a child's life.

Though I was blessed to have my father for 16 years of my life, I will never forget the pain and agony I experienced when he died, and the impact that his absence had on my life.

My father's absence left a hole in my soul. I was angry and sorrowful, which was instrumental in me going down a path of self-destructive behavior. At the time of this book's release, I have been without my father for 53 years. Five decades missing my daddy has been almost too much to handle.

And though there were a lot of negative effects of him being absent, I want you to know that I have survived the struggles and issues surrounding fatherlessness, and the main reason is because God became the Father to my fatherlessness.

As you read this book, I hope the brokenness caused by the absence of a father may be healed. I hope the wounds that have followed many through life will be mended, and that men will be guided to be the fathers that God called them to be, and that their children need them to be.

Where It All Began

On Thursday, August 5, 1971, I was in Mount Sinai Hospital in Cleveland, Ohio, with my sister Shirley, watching my father in a hospital bed as he lay motionless because of a cerebral hemorrhage. By that point, my father had been on kidney dialysis for two years and was now on his seventh day in the hospital. He was non-responsive and breathing intermittently. At 3:00 p.m. on that day, my father took one last deep breath in my presence. I went around the corner to the nurse's station and told them that I think my father just died. A group of doctors and nurses rushed into the room and 15 minutes later, they exited his room and told me, "Your father is dead."

For the next three hours, all I could do was cry. A week later, I was standing with my family at Crown Hill Cemetery in Indianapolis, Indiana and watched as his casket was lowered into a grave. I began to tremble and shake, and I cried hysterically as the casket disappeared out of my sight.

My father was gone. He would be absent the rest of my life. And though his absence wasn't intentional, deliberate, or willful, it affected me in the same way a father's absence affects his child, especially his son.

1. I had no one to teach me about manhood as I was approaching that stage in my life.
2. I had no adult male to be a restraining force in my life.
3. I would wrestle and struggle with abandonment issues throughout my life.
4. I was absolutely finished with God, because I blamed God for my father no longer being around for me! Why would I ever want to have anything to do with God again?

I had the same attitude about God that Pharaoh had when Moses approached him about letting God's people go to hold a feast to God in the wilderness.

Read Pharaoh's response:

"And Pharaoh said, Who is the Lord, that I should obey his voice to let Israel go? I know not the Lord, neither will I let Israel go." Exodus 5:2 (KJV)

Pharaoh did three things:

Pharaoh **rejected** God's appeal.

Pharaoh **renounced** any acknowledgment of God.

Pharaoh **rebelled** against God's authority.

Like Pharaoh I did not want to hear what God had to say: "Who is the Lord, that I should obey his voice…"

(Rejected God)

Like Pharaoh I did not want to have anything to do with God: "I know not the Lord."

(Renounced God)

Like Pharaoh I was not going to obey God: "…neither will I let Israel go."

(Rebelled against God)

And from that day forth, my father would be missing from my life forever. I went through life rejecting God, renouncing God, and rebelling against God, because if God was any good, He would not have taken my father from me.

This disregard for the Lord that I had was a result of my anger, hurt, and resentment toward God because I blamed him for my father's death, my father's absence! The pain and anger that I had manifested itself in my life in the form of alcohol and drug abuse, unhealthy relationships, harmful sexual behavior, and other destructive and abusive behaviors that impacted not only myself, but others as well.

Finally, during my downward plunge, the Lord Jesus Christ came into my life and rescued me and began a process of healing and nurturing in my life. Though I am still "under construction," God continues to peel back the layers of scar tissue on my heart, restore my soul, and heal me from the inside out.

Little by little, the Lord has done for me what I could not do for myself!

> *"He restoreth my soul." (Ps. 23:3a, KJV)*

So, why another book on fatherlessness?

The purpose of this book is to initiate a REBOOT in the lives of some fathers.

In this world of computers, cell phones, cable, and satellite TV, every now and then something goes wrong in the operating system. When the system is failing to operate properly, one of the first things technical support tells you to do is to "reboot" the system. In other words, shut it down and restart the device. There are men out here today who have failed to operate properly in their role as a father because they have been absent in the lives of their children. What they need to do is "reboot" by starting over again in proper working order as a father.

I pray this book, *The Reboot*, will accomplish three things in the lives of men who need a reboot when it comes to their relationship with their children. Those three things are:

To Help men understand how fatherlessness impacts a child, and to realize what their God given responsibilities as a father requires.

To Heal broken relationships between fathers and their children, and by doing so, allows healing to take place in their individual lives.

To Head fathers to a restored or saving relationship with the Lord Jesus Christ.

Then Jesus said, "Come to me, all of you who are weary and carry heavy burdens, and I will give you rest. Take my yoke upon you. Let me teach you, because I am humble and gentle, and you will find rest for your souls. For my yoke is easy to bear, and the burden I give you is light." Matthew 11:28-30, NLT.

My prayer is that the Lord uses this book to do great things in the lives of fathers and children all over this nation. I pray that He uses this book to motivate men to **rescue and restore** their children! If anything great comes from this small piece of work, it will be truly because God has blessed it to happen, but remember, God is in the business of doing great things with just a little.

It was with a rod that Moses stretched out his hand and God divided the Red Sea.

It was from a rock that God supplied water to the over 2 million Israelites leaving Egypt.

It was with a sling and a stone in the hand of a young David that God brought down a giant warrior.

It was with Gideon and just 300 men that God brought down thousands of Midianites.

It was with the lunch of a little boy that the Lord fed thousands who were hungry.

It was with some spittle and dust that the Lord restored the sight of a blind man.

It was with the birth of a little baby named Jesus that God introduced salvation to the world.

Ephesians 3:20 "Now unto him that is able to do exceeding abundantly above all that we ask or think, according to the power that worketh in us…" **(KJV)**

God can do great things with just a little!

FATHERS, LET'S REBOOT!

Chapter 1

"I DON'T HAVE A FATHER"

One day when I was in the grocery store, I happened upon a woman who I knew was the aunt of a young man who was fathered out of wedlock by one of my closest friends. When I asked her how her nephew was doing (we'll call him William), she informed me that William was living on his own and engaged to be married. When I asked her if William had heard from his father recently, she uttered, "William says, 'I don't have a father!'" Those five little words sent chills through my body. Those five little words made the hairs on the back of my neck stand. Those five little words drove a stake into the very depths of my heart. Those five little words exposed an issue that has, and is having a devastating effect on our families in part and in society. That issue is "absent fathers."

"I don't have a father!"

These are the words that express the anger and frustration of many young boys in our society today.

"I don't have a father!"

These are the words that reveal the pain and trauma of many young girls in our world today.

"I don't have a father!"

These are the words that speak to the rejection, the hurt, the abandonment, and the suffering of many young men and women who have had to experience the reality of a life without a father in it. An **"absent father."**

"I don't have a father!"

These are the words that communicate with stinging veracity, and results in much dysfunction in the lives of numerous children and adults who have been devastated by this phenomenon of "absent fathers."

The reality is that everyone has a biological father, but not everyone has had a father in their lives. That daddy who loves them, provides for them, protects, nurtures, and disciplines them. The type of fathers who are called to be in the lives of their children are much more than a father by name.

Dr. James Dobson makes the following assertion in his book *Straight Talk to Men and their Wives:* {1}

"The Western world stands at a great crossroad in its history. It is my opinion that our very survival as a people will depend upon the presence or absence of masculine leadership in millions of homes."

"I don't have a father!"

William's denial of his father was a response to his father's absence, an absence that caused him to feel rejected by his father. William's emotional scars caused by the abandonment of his father resulted in William casting aside any acknowledgment of, or a desire to have a paternal relationship in his life.

I have worked in the criminal justice system for approximately 28 years as both a probation officer and a bailiff on the municipal, state, and federal levels. I have interviewed hundreds of defendants and written just as many investigative reports for judges in my career. I cannot tell you the number of times I have interviewed a young man, and when inquiring about his family history he tells me, **"I don't have a father!"**

I have been in Christian ministry for over 30 years. At least 25 of those years were spent serving in pastoral ministry as a youth pastor, an assistant pastor, or senior pastor of a church. I have sat down with angry young men whose single mothers, at their wits end, brought their child to me in hopes that I might be able to help her with her child's behavioral problems. When talking to these young men and inquiring about their relationship with their father, they look at me with hurt, humiliation, and hostility in their eyes and respond with, **"I don't have a father!"**

I was in my kindergarten class one day when a few of us were talking about our fathers. Suddenly one little boy said that he didn't have a father. I didn't understand what he was saying at the time because I knew everyone has a father. In my naiveté, I didn't realize he wasn't saying that he didn't have a biological father, but that he didn't have a father in his life.

Right now, you might be experiencing some anger and pain as you reflect on your own life and the absence of a father in it. That means you are getting in touch with your feelings and hopefully headed for a breakthrough in your life.

Keep reading. Don't quit before the miracle happens.

~ Journal ~

Chapter 2

"HOW COME HE DON'T WANT ME?"

The *Fresh Prince of Bel-Air* is a sitcom starring Will Smith. It is about a young African American male from West Philadelphia, who is being raised in a single parent household by his mother. He is sent to Bel-Air, California to live with his successful and wealthy uncle, aunt, and their children. This is to save him from the streets of his own neighborhood in Philly.

In one famous episode, Will's father, Lou, who ran out on him and his mother 14 years earlier, comes to visit Will while passing through on one of his runs as a cross country truck driver. Lou spends an entire day at an amusement park with Will and gets his hopes built up when he offers to let Will spend the summer traveling with him across the country. {1}

In the closing scene of that episode, Lou disappoints Will by going back on his invitation to spend the summer together on the road. When Lou leaves, Will's uncle Phil tries to console his young nephew, who is trying to make it appear as though he was not fazed by what happened. Finally, Will's true feelings come out as he states the following:

"It ain't like I'm still five years old."

"Ain't like I'm going to be sitting up every night asking mommy when's daddy coming home."

"Hey, he wasn't there to teach me how to shoot my first basket, but I learned."

"Got through my first date without him."

"I learned to drive without him."

"Learned how to shave without him."

"Learned how to fight without him"

"I had 14 great birthdays without him and he never even sent me a card."

To hell with him!"

"I didn't need him then and I don't need him now."

"I'm gonna get through college without him."

"I'm gonna get a great job without him."

"I'm gonna marry a beautiful honey (woman) and have a whole bunch of kids."

"I'm gonna be a better father then he ever was, and I sure as hell don't need him for that cause ain't a damn thing he could ever teach me about how to love my kid."

In that final, agonizing moment, Will breaks down crying and asks his uncle Phil:

"HOW COME HE DON'T WANT ME MAN?"

"How come he don't want me" is another way of asking the question that is on the heart and mind of every child who has been the victim of abandonment and rejection of a father. Through the searing pain of his heart wrenching outcry, Will asks the question that millions of young men and women wrestle with all their lives. The question that fills eyes with tears. The question that leaves hearts broken. The question that pierces to the depths of the soul, leaving children both young and old shattered, crippled, and scared! And that question is:

"How Come He Don't Want Me?"

When a child believes his father doesn't want him, in essence he is saying, *"My father doesn't value me, my father doesn't think I'm important, my father doesn't think I matter, my father doesn't love me."*

God looks at children as something special and precious that He is giving to the parents. **Psalm 127:3 says,**

"Children are a gift from the LORD; they are a reward from him." **(NLT2)**

It says that God looks at children as a *"gift"* and a *"reward."* Often when we receive something from someone, we say that person, *"blessed me"* with whatever it was. Children are God's blessing to parents, and such fathers (and mothers) ought to treat their children like the blessings they are: God's gift to them.

When a father abandons and rejects his child, often the child's first response after the hurt and pain is anger. The Bible warns us about the effects of driving our children to anger. **Colossians 3:21 says this:**

"Fathers, provoke not your children to anger, lest they be discouraged."

That word *discourage* can be translated, "to lose heart," or "to crush their spirit." When a father drives his children to anger by being absent in their lives, he literally can "crush their spirit" and cause them to "lose heart."

Children with a crushed spirit, who have lost heart, often go through life with a defeated attitude. They have no hope that their lives can get any better and believe that life is not worth living.

One day, I was at work in the court where a woman was being sentenced in a case where she had been convicted of being excessive in her corporal discipline of her teenage son. He was in the courtroom in tears and overwhelmed with guilt because the incident originated from him under-achieving as a student. He was a former honors student and varsity athlete, but his grades had dropped to the point where he had become ineligible to play sports. He wasn't doing his class work or homework and had been cutting classes. His attitude had become rebellious at home and the people he had been associating with were counterproductive to his future.

When I had the opportunity to talk to him about these drastic changes occurring, the tears continued to flow as he told me what was going on in his life. His biological father, who he never had any relationship with was in jail. His adopted father, who had separated from his mother several years earlier, had become uninvolved in his life.

This young man was angry, hurt, and lost. He confessed that he had no adult male to guide him through that phase of his life. It was apparent that his anger concerning his father being absent in his life was the root of the problems he was experiencing.

On another occasion, while serving in the capacity of youth pastor at our church, I became aware of a young man who seemed to be causing his mother great distress. He was about sixteen years old and came to our teen bible study under duress. He came up through our youth ministry prior to, and during his teenage years and was extremely intelligent. According to his mother, he had developed a behavioral problem.

At her request, I tried spending time talking to him during our youth meetings, but I didn't make any headway with him. During our conversations, he attempted to bait me into arguments concerning the reality of God, and the authenticity of the Bible. When he would become involved in horseplay with the other teenage boys, you could see that his intent was to try and hurt them. He began wearing black clothing and seemed to be embracing the Gothic subculture. He became increasingly rebellious and withdrew from all adults. Eventually, I learned from his mother that his father was not involved in his life. I got a sense from her that the absence of his father in his life left him angry, undisciplined, combative, and feeling unloved by his father. As hard as I tried to connect with him, he would not allow that to happen. The last time I saw him, he was in court facing felony burglary charges.

The reality is that **"FATHERS MATTER"** in the lives of their children. The pain and anger a young man and a young woman feel when his or her father abandons them is a reality I have not only witnessed in my personal experiences, in both the church and the court, but it is also seen in the Word of God. Read the story of Ishmael:

"Early the next morning Abraham took some food and a skin of water and gave them to Hagar. He set them on her shoulders and then sent her off with the boy. She went on her way and wandered in the desert of Bathsheba. When the water in the skin was gone, she put the boy under one of the bushes. Then she went off and sat down nearby, about a bowshot away, for she thought, "I cannot watch the boy die." And as she sat there nearby, she began to sob. **God heard the boy crying,"** **(Genesis 21:14-17a, NIV)**

Ishmael was approximately 16 years old when he was cast out by his father. The Bible says that "God heard the boy crying." Was he crying because the provisions of food and water had run out? Was he crying because of his fear of being in the desert? Was he crying at the thought that he and his mother would die in the desert, or was he crying because his father had cast him aside and the pain of being abandoned by his father, and the feeling of being unloved by his father was too much for him to bear?

How many young boys and girls are crying right now?

Crying because they've been rejected by their daddy.

Crying because they've been abandoned by their daddy.

Crying because they have no relationship with their daddy.

Crying because they don't know a daddy's love.

Crying because they don't feel a daddy's touch.

Crying because they bear the pain of not having daddy in their lives.

The following observation is made by someone I know:

"Parent's Guide to The Spiritual Mentoring of Teens." {2}

Veteran youth worker Joe White reports that in his 30 years of counseling troubled teens, he has made a habit of asking boys who are rebelling or in serious trouble, *"How is your relationship with your dad?" And most always the answer comes back, "I don't know my dad" or "What dad?" or, "I never see my dad."* **(Chapter 6, pg 84)**

I am not trying to presuppose that every problem a young person has rests on their father's presence and involvement in their life, but there is enough evidence for one to conclude that many problems concerning drugs, abuse, teenage pregnancy, runaways, incarceration, violence, sexual abuse, behavioral and emotional issues find their roots in the absence of a father in his child's life.

"How Come He Don't Want Me?"

~ Journal ~

Chapter 3

"WHAT HAPPENS WHEN FATHERS AREN'T AROUND"

I have never been one who likes to spend a whole lot of time quoting statistics when trying to make a point, but in this instance, I believe that the phenomenon of absent fathers is so critically important it is worth me bearing out some data to show **what happens when daddy's not around.**

The following information is from the National Fatherhood Initiative in Philadelphia, PA, and was posted on their website in 2022 {1}

When fathers are absent in the home and life of a child, children are at greater risk for the following:

- Four times at greater risk of poverty
- More likely to have behavioral problems
- Two times greater risk of infant mortality
- More likely to go to prison
- More likely to commit crime
- Seven times more likely to become pregnant as a teen
- More likely to face abuse and neglect

- More likely to abuse drugs and alcohol
- Two times more likely to suffer obesity
- Two times more likely to drop out of school

Author Anthony Campolo in his book, *It's Friday, But Sunday's Comin'* refers to a concept by Charles H. Cooley, Dean of American Sociology called the **"Looking Glass Self."** Cooley says this:

"A person's self-concept is established by what he/she thinks the most important persons in his/her life think of him/her." {2} (Chap 3, pg. 27)

If this is true, then how a child views themselves is critically influenced by how their parents view them. If a father is not in his child's life, then it may seem the child is not important to the father. If the child feels that they are not important to one of the most important people in their life, they will conclude that they are not important at all.

But, according to the National Fatherhood Initiative, there is a drastic difference when a father is present and involved in the life of their children.

When fathers are present in the life of a child, children:

- Have a lower rate of infant mortality
- Have a lower risk of low birth rate
- Experience less emotional and behavioral problems
- Experience less of a chance to encounter neglect and abuse
- Have lower rates of injury
- Have lower rates of obesity
- Achieve higher school performance
- Have less incidence of teen pregnancy
- Are less likely to be incarcerated as a juvenile
- Experience less alcohol and substance abuse problems

- Are involved in less criminal activity
- Are less likely to commit suicide

From my experiences in working in the court and working in ministry, I have seen the effects of not having a father in their lives can produce.

I have seen young boys grow up to be angry and bitter young men who turn to self-destructive behavior as their outlet, when a father is absent in their lives. Falling into alcohol and drug addiction and turning to criminal activity and violence are all manifestations rooted in the fact that their father was not there for them.

When a father is absent in the lives of young girls, I have seen them grow up to be emotionally needy young women, with a hole in their soul. They try to fill that hole with men who aren't their fathers. I've also seen those young women enter dysfunctional and abusive relationships and stay in them because they are trying to fill a hole that an absent father has left them. They use their unhealthy relationships to try and heal that "father wound" and it never happens.

When fathers are present in a child's life, they are able to give that child some essentials for their mental well-being. What are those essentials?

A father's attention.

A father's acknowledgment.

A father's affection.

A father's affirmation.

If you want mental and emotional wellness in your child's life, it is critical that these four things are an integral part of your relationship with your child.

These four things also tell your child that you love them. If you talk to many adolescents and teenagers today, the one thing they will tell you they're missing is the feeling of being loved.

We see an example of these four things at work in the relationship of Jesus and His Heavenly Father seen in the Gospel of **Matthew 3:13-17 (ESV)**:

> *"Then Jesus came from Galilee to the Jordan to John, to be baptized by him.*
>
> *14 John would have prevented him, saying, "I need to be baptized by you, and do you come to me?"*
>
> *15 But Jesus answered him, "Let it be so now, for thus it is fitting for us to fulfill all righteousness." Then he consented.*
>
> *16 And when Jesus was baptized, immediately he went up from the water, and behold, the heavens were opened to him, and he saw the Spirit of God descending like a dove and coming to rest on Him;*
>
> *17 and behold, a voice from heaven said, "This is my beloved Son, with whom I am well pleased."*

In these four verses, we see the application of the aforementioned principles:

The Father's Attention

> *"the Spirit of God descending like a dove and coming to rest on him;"*

The father's presence was with his son as His spirit rested on Jesus. The way a father gives his child attention is to be in his child's presence. It's spending time with the child that makes the child feel loved.

The Father's Acknowledgment

> *"This is my beloved Son,"*

"My" is a powerful word. It acknowledges that the object of the word *"My"* belongs to the one speaking. Many children do not feel acknowledged by their father because their father is absent in their life. They feel discarded and deserted. A child needs to hear his father say, *"This is my son, this is my daughter."*

The Father's Affection

> *"My beloved Son,"*

The word *beloved* means "dearly loved or well loved." It is a term of great affection and delight. The Heavenly Father is expressing how greatly He loves and delights in His Son Jesus. A child needs to know how much his or her father loves and delights in them, that his love for them is precious and special.

Jesus told His disciples in **John 15:9**

"As the Father hath loved me, so have I loved you."

The Father's Affirmation

"with whom I am well pleased."

When you affirm someone, you speak positively about that person directly to them or in the presence of others. Too many times we tear our children down with negative words and criticisms instead of building them up with positive words. The Bible says, "Death and life are in the power of the tongue" **(Proverbs 18:21 KJV)**. We need to speak life into our children.

When fathers aren't around, another pivotal function is missing that is so needed in a child's life as they grow older, especially in a boy. Fathers need to be around to "ARREST" certain behaviors in their child. I will speak more to this in a later chapter but let me take a moment to explain what I mean.

Fathers Arrest Bad Behaviors In Their Children

When I was 10 years old, we lived in Los Angeles, California. My mother was a nurse, and my father worked for VJ Record Company as a road manager for singer Joe Simon. As a road manager, my father was constantly away from home.

At the time, the Watts riots had erupted in Los Angeles and the National Guard had been dispatched to LA. All along the streets of Crenshaw were armed soldiers and armored vehicles. To a 10-year-old boy, that was exciting. My mother and I were at the Crenshaw Shopping Plaza on Saturday afternoon. After picking up groceries, she wanted to get home ASAP and away from all the armed soldiers because she recognized the potential danger even though her 10-year-old son didn't.

When it was time to go, I didn't want to leave, I wanted to watch the soldiers. My mother told me if I didn't come home, she was going to leave. I told her she could leave, and I would walk home. Please understand, I was 10 years old. I was, as the old folks would say, "smelling myself," and my dad was not around because he was down south touring with Joe Simon. So, my mom left and after about an hour, I made the two mile walk to our home.

I went to bed that night. When I opened my eyes the next morning, my father was standing over me with a belt in his hand. He said to me, "What's this I hear that you don't have to listen to what your mother says?" It was at that point the correction (whooping) began and my mother never had that problem with me again.

Proverbs 22:15 says, *"Foolishness is bound up in the heart of a child; The rod of discipline will remove it far from him."* **(NASB)**

That is why fathers need to have a relationship with their children. Fathers are to be an arresting force in their lives. They should not only discipline their children, but share with them what God says, so that the rules they lay down according to God's Word will be followed by them. Just know that without a relationship with them, your rules will mean little or nothing.

"Rules without Relationship lead to Rebellion." {3}

Dr. Adrian Rogers

Fathers need to be around to not only give attention to their child, acknowledge their child, show affection to their child, and affirm their child, but to arrest certain behaviors of their child.

Good News Even If Your Father Is Absent!

Your earthly father may be absent in your life. Your earthly father may not have shown you love. But there is a Heavenly Father who is there for you.

He's known as God the Father, and He will always be attentive to you, acknowledge you, show you affection, and affirm you.

Psalm 68:5 calls Him a *"Father to the fatherless."*

God can fill every void in your life caused by the absence of a father, but God's perfect will is for fathers to be fathers to their children, and that means fathers being around and active in the lives of their children.

~ Journal ~

Chapter 4

"LIKE FATHER LIKE SON"

Too often, this phenomenon of fatherlessness is passed down from one generation to the next. It is a cycle that is sometimes perpetuated by an absent grandfather, which is passed on to a father, which is passed on to a son.

It is like alcoholism that runs through generations of a family. It is like criminal incarceration that runs through generations of a family. It is like poverty that runs through generations of a family.

And with all these generational curses, the **"cycle must be broken."** Far too often we see dysfunctional behavior and mindsets that are passed down from generation to generation that leave family member after family member defeated and devastated.

The Bible gives us instances where sons continued in the same evil paths as their fathers.

King Abijam

"In the eighteenth year of King Jeroboam the son of Nebat, Abijam became king over Judah… 3 And he walked in all the sins of his father, which he had done before him; his heart was not loyal to the LORD his God." **1 Kings 15:1, 3 (NKJV)**

King Nadab

"Now Nadab the son of Jeroboam became king over Israel in the second year of Asa king of Judah, and he reigned over Israel two years. 26 And he did evil in the sight of the LORD, and walked in the way of his father, and in his sin by which he had made Israel sin." **1 Kings 15:25-26 (NKJV)**

King Amon

"Amon was twenty-two years old when he became king, and he reigned two years in Jerusalem. 22 But he did evil in the sight of the LORD, as his father Manasseh had done;" **2 Chronicles 33:21-22 (NKJV)**

King Jehoahaz

"Jehoahaz was twenty-three years old when he became king, and he reigned three months in Jerusalem...... 32 And he did evil in the sight of the LORD, according to all that his fathers had done." **2 Kings 23:31-32 (NKJV)**

King Ahaziah

"Ahaziah the son of Ahab became king over Israel in Samaria in the seventeenth year of Jehoshaphat king of Judah, and reigned two years over Israel......52 He did evil in the sight of the LORD, and walked in the way of his father" **1 Kings 22:51-52 (NKJV)**

All these kings continued the cycle of sin like their fathers, and it not only had an impact on their families, but also on the nations of God's people.

As we saw earlier, fatherlessness not only affects the families from generation to generation, but it also affects the nation (crime, drugs, mental health, etc.)

"Like father, like son!"

How often have we heard stories of mothers who had a divorce, or a bad breakup, and in the heat of their anger with something their son may have done, they've said these inflammatory words, **"You're just like your daddy?"**

"Like father, like son!"

Not always, but in many cases the mother is right. The son has picked up some ugly attitudes, bad behaviors, or harmful habits that were passed down from the father, and now she is re-living it through her son.

"Like father, like son!"

In **Genesis chapters 12 and 20**, Abraham deceived the Pharaoh of Egypt, and King Abimelech of Gerar respectively, in believing that his beautiful wife Sarah was his sister because he was afraid that these rulers would desire to have her and kill him knowing he was her husband.

In **Genesis chapter 26**, Abraham's adult son Isaac deceived Philistines men and King Abimelech of Gerar in believing that his wife Rebekah was his sister because he was afraid that the Philistines and the King would desire to have her and kill him knowing he was her husband.

"Like father, like son!"

Throughout the Bible we see that old adage, *"the fruit doesn't fall far from the tree"* realized when it comes to fathers and sons.

"Like father, like son!"

David was the greatest king in the history of Israel yet fell short when it came to being a father. But his shortcomings as a father showed up in the lives of his children.

How often do we see men so busy trying to be successful in the world, in business, at their jobs, that they fail as a father because they are absent in the lives of their children?

Unfortunately, I've even witnessed this in the church. I've seen men with positions in the church dedicate more time to their position than to their family. Pastors who were so busy being "Mr. Pastor" that they failed as a parent. Deacons who were so busy being "Mr. Deacon" that they failed as a parent.

What often happens is either their children are running amuck and constantly getting arrested, or are on drugs because daddy is not there to discipline them and reign them in. It is because daddy has put his position before his children. And in many instances, their children turn from God and the church because they see the hypocrisy. Their father is there for church and everybody else, but not for them.

"Some may disagree, but when I was a pastor, my motto was, 'After God, family first, then ministry.'"

That was David's problem. He put being a king before being a parent. But that wasn't David's only problem. King David's inordinate uncontrolled lustful passions would be relived in the lives of his sons Amnon, Absalom, and Solomon.

David's son Amnon raped his half-sister, Tamar. David's son Absalom would go on and kill his half-brother Amnon and betray his father. His father refused to deal with Amnon, and eventually Absalom stole his father David's kingdom from him, and in an act of contempt for his father, slept with his father's concubines.

In the **Life Application Bible's** profile of Absalom, the following analysis is made:

"A father's mistakes are often reflected in the lives of his children. In Absalom, David saw a bitter replay and amplification of many of his past sins." {1}

How could a son treat his own father with such disrespect and contempt? The answer may lie here. In two Samuel chapters 2-12, you never hear Absalom, or the rest of his children mentioned. That is a period of nineteen years. But during that time, David was busy being king, fighting the Philistines, trying to retrieve the ark, engaged in battle with the Ammonites and Syrians, and chasing after Bathsheba.

David was too busy being king to be a father, and his life became the pattern for his children.

"Like father, like son!"

How a son often thinks, how he acts, and what his core beliefs are, often pattern after their father's.

In the movie **Gladiator,** the aging Emperor Marcus Aurelius is about to hand over the reins of his power to his loyal general Maximus instead of his son Commodus. Commodus, the emperor's son, is a self-centered tyrant who is lusting after his own sister. Marcus Aurelius says something profound to his son on why he is not appointing him as his successor to the throne. He says, **"your faults as a son, are my failures as a father."** {2}

A young man drank himself to death by the age of 34. His father's drinking was the leading cause of his own death at the age of 52. The father's favorite saying was, *"I wanna live fast, die young, and make a pretty corpse."* In the last few years of the son's life as both family and friends tried to convince him that his drinking was killing him, he stated, *"I want to be like my father, I wanna live fast, die young, and make a pretty corpse."* And just like his father, he did!

In the movie **The General's Daughter** (which we will give a more detailed synopsis of later), John Travolta plays a character named Paul Brennan who is investigating the death of a general's daughter. While questioning a suspect, Brennen is asked, *"Did you love your father?"* Brennen's response was, *"My father was a gambler, a drunk, and a womanizer...I worshiped him!"* {3}

Whether it's living fast, dying young, and making a pretty corpse, or whether it's worshiping a gambler, a drunk, or a womanizer, in many cases the result is the same ...

"Like father, like son!"

Please understand that fathers can be one of the greatest influences in their children's life, but it means just that, being in their children's life. Fathers who are in their children's lives and are intentional about training up their children in the way they

should go set the positive patterns for their children.

In his commentary on the Gospel of Matthew, John McArthur speaks to this point when expounding on the life of Andrew Murray, the great Christian pastor and author. McArthur shares the following:

> *"Andrew Murray lived an exceptionally holy life. Among those on whom his influence was the greatest were his children and grandchildren. Five of his six sons became ministers of the gospel and four of his daughter's became minister's wives. Ten grandsons became ministers, and thirteen grandchildren became missionaries."* {4}

Author Henry Blackaby tells of the spiritual impact his father had on the patterns of his life:

> *"As a child, I observed my father's love for God's Word and was deeply impressed by the fact that he found such delight in the studying of the Bible. Watching my father, I came to know from earliest memory that spending time with God in His Word must be the most important endeavor of life. And so it was that I set my heart on a course to know God more intimately too."* {5}

(Encounters with God, Transforming Your Bible Study, pg. v, foreword)

As fathers, what we don't want in the life of our children is:

    Our habits to become their hindrances…

    Our follies to become their frailties…

    Our faults to become their failures…

    Our shortcomings to become their stumbling blocks…

    Our sins playing out in the scenarios of their lives…

In 1974, Harry Chapin sung a song about the relationship between a father and a son. The name of the song is, "Cat's In The Cradle." The sobering lyrics of this song demonstrate how a son can take after his father. {6}

The song tells a story about a son and a father from the birth of the son until the son himself grows up and has children.

From the time the son is born, to the age of 10 years old, until before the child graduates from college, the father seems too preoccupied with work and other things in life to spend the time with his son that his son so desperately wants and needs. Every time the father tells the son the unfortunate news that he doesn't have time for him right now but they would get together soon and have a good time then. And every time the father would say that, the son would say he was going to be just like his father.

When the son graduates from college he stops by the home and his father acknowledges how proud he is of his son's accomplishments and asks him to sit a while. Unfortunately, the son has something else to do and asks his father to borrow his car.

Finally the father has retired and his son now has a family of his own. Time has passed and the father hasn't seen his son in a while. He calls his son and tells him that he'd like to see him if he could find time. The son tells his father how busy he is with his job and the kids but it was sure nice talking to him. It's at this point that the father realizes that his son has turned out just like him.

There is a scripture in the Bible that speaks to how the sins of a father often passes down from one generation to the next generation. God will allow the sins, faults, habits, and their consequences to pass from generation to generation. This is why so often we see children repeating the same sins, faults, and habits of their parents. This is why the phrase "like father like son" becomes a reality in the lives of our children. **Numbers 14:18** puts it this way,

"GOD, slow to get angry and huge in loyal love, forgiving iniquity and rebellion and sin; Still, never just whitewashing sin. But extending the fallout of parents' sins to children into the third, even the fourth generation." **(MSG)**

Sons often grow up thinking and behaving just like their fathers, repeating and reliving the same negatives patterns of their fathers.

"Like father, like son!"

~ Journal ~

Chapter 5

"HEROES"

What is a Hero?

A hero is someone you admire for their achievements, abilities, qualities, and strengths.

Growing up in the 60's and 70's, most of the guys I hung around with had heroes, and most of our heroes were from the field of sports. I had my heroes also.

In football, my heroes were Jim Brown and Johnny Unitas. In baseball, my heroes were Willie Mays and Mickey Mantle, and in basketball my heroes were Earl "The Pearl" Monroe and Julius "Dr. J" Erving.

If you were to ask young people today who their hero is they may tell you some rap or hip-hop artist, some music mogul or producer, or some billionaire.

But my number one hero growing up was my father.

In September 2007, I had the opportunity to participate in a "power luncheon" at a local church. The luncheon was sponsored by their men's fellowship ministry. **The theme of the luncheon was "He-**

roes." One of the speakers was a former NFL player who had won two Super Bowls. Another speaker was a pastor of a mega church in North Carolina. I and a few other pastors facilitated several of the breakout groups. As each speaker focused on the theme and began to testify about the "heroes" in their life, I began to think about the man who was my first "hero."

My father was my hero!

Yes, my father was my "hero." From my earliest recollection, I always looked up to and admired my father. I loved him tremendously. He was the one who taught me how to ride a bike, catch a football, how to block and tackle, and how to hit a baseball. My father was the one who taught me how to swim, shoot pool, play chess, wrestle, box, and drive a car. He came to watch me wrestle and was at my baseball and football games. When the older and bigger kids would bully us younger and smaller kids, my father would come to our rescue.

The kids in the neighborhood admired my father because he spent time with us. He coached Peewee League football and was a lifeguard at a neighborhood recreation center. He showed us how to play four corners, and when we had water hose nights, he'd be in the midst of us getting soaked.

My father grew up in the streets of Indianapolis, and he was drawn to that life. When I was a child, he would hang out on the corner with his friends, and at the bars on Saturday (all day). I was by his side, just like in today's world. Fathers spend time with their sons at sport bars and tailgating events (at times it was exciting). Though it was not the environment my mother wanted for me, it didn't matter to me as long as I was with my father. I loved to be with him, and he loved to be with me!

Then one day a cruel thing happened. My father died!

Heroes die! What do you do when your "hero" dies? What happens when your "hero" is no longer there?

When a young boy is accustomed to having a "hero" in his life and that "hero" is no longer there, that young boy looks for another "hero." After my father's death, it was the older boys who became my new "heroes." They were the ones who were cool. They seemed to have it going on. They were the ones I began to look up to. It was the older boys who were drinking wine on the street corners. It was the older boys in the alleys shooting craps. It was the older boys in the park selling marijuana. It was the older boys in the barber shop who were smoking, cursing, and telling the younger boys about their sexual exploits and advising us on sex. The older boys told us how to respond when you get caught cheating on your girlfriend. They even bragged about how many kids they had (who by the way they were not taking care of or hadn't see in weeks, months, or years). And to me and many other young boys without a "hero" in their lives, these older boys became our definition of a man. These older guys became what manhood was all about. And these older boys became the new "heroes."

The legacy of a hero!

A year before my father died, he told me that he had joined a church and was getting baptized. As a child in Indianapolis, Indiana, my father had given his life to Christ. Now at the age of 52, with failing health due to high blood pressure, and on dialysis because of kidney disease, my father must have known that his time on this earth was short. He recommitted his life to Jesus Christ and was baptized.

Being baptized signified that my father was dying to that old sinful life and rising to a new life in Jesus Christ! It was an outward sign of an inward change.

At age fifteen, it did not mean a whole lot to me at the time, but when I had my own personal experience with Jesus Christ, I realized that my father's actions years earlier had planted a seed that would one day take root, grow, and bloom into my decision to receive Jesus

Christ as my Lord and Savior. What my father had left me was a legacy, a **"legacy of faith."**

That was the great legacy of my "hero," my faith in Jesus Christ!

The Lord Jesus Christ is my hero!

Once I received Jesus as my Savior and Lord and realized He didn't just save me from God's wrath because of my sins, but also forgave me for my sins. The Lord became my new "hero!"

Jesus Christ is a "hero" that loved you so much that He died for you. He is a "hero" that has reunited us with the Heavenly Father (God). He is a "hero" who has placed His divine presence (the Holy Spirit) into your body. He is a "hero" who has promised a place called heaven for those who have received Him. Anyone who has done all that for you is truly a "hero."

Jesus is my "hero." I hope you have or will make Him yours!

When I was growing up, I used to watch a lot of westerns. As a matter of fact, even though I became hooked on sports, to this day there is nothing on the television that I enjoy watching more than a good "shoot-'em-up" cowboy movie. My favorite character in the westerns was not the outlaw, but the good guy, the "hero."

- The hero was the good guy.
- The hero was the one that came when there was trouble.
- The hero was the one that came to the rescue in the nick of time.
- The hero was the one who saved the day.
- The hero was the one who restored order.
- The hero was the one who got the girl in the end.
- And the hero was the one who often gave his own life to save others.

And Jesus is much like the "hero" of those old-time westerns:

➤ Jesus is the only one born good and without sin.

➤ Jesus was the one who came when mankind was in trouble.

➤ Jesus is the one who rescued mankind from the wrath of God's punishment for sin.

➤ Jesus is the one who saved the day by bringing salvation to the world.

➤ Jesus is the one who restored the believers to right relationship with God.

➤ Jesus is the one who got the girl, the Church, the Bride of Christ

➤ And Jesus was the one who gave His life that other might be saved.

For those of you fathers who do not have a relationship with your child, it's not too late. You can still become a **"hero"** in their lives, and in their eyes. Let me share with you a couple of concepts that can help guide you to be the **"hero"** your child needs, wants, and deserves.

Jesus is the Savior of the world.... Jesus is the world's hero.

When it comes to fathers and their children, it's important and imperative that fathers are their heroes. But a hero can't be a hero if he's not around. Heroes must be present to be heroes, and there are several things heroes must do for their children.

"Heroes rescue and restore their children!"

~ Journal ~

Chapter 6

HEROES 'RESCUE' THEIR CHILDREN

"If I could offer a single prescription for the survival of America, and particularly black America, it would be to restore the family. And if you asked me how to do it, my answer (doubtlessly oversimplified) would be: 'Save the boys.'"
(William Raspberry, a black columnist with the Washington Post — July 18, 1989)

The Derrick Redmond Story

It was the 1992 Summer Olympics Games in Barcelona, Spain. Derrick Redmond from Great Britain was running in the 400-meter event and was favored to win. He had trained hard and sacrificed much over the past four years preparing for this race. As he was coming around the backstretch, his hamstring snapped. He tried desperately to finish the race, but his injury was so bad and the pain so severe that he couldn't walk. Derrick tried to hop to the finish line on one leg, but it was to no avail. All of a sudden his father, who was in the stadium, ran down from section 131. When the security guards tried to stop him, he pushed his way through them, leaped over the rail, and ran onto the track. When he reached his son, he told Derrick to just lay there until the medical personnel arrived. Derrick told his father that he didn't come this far not to finish the race. Derrick's father said, "Then we'll finish it together," and as Derrick hopped on one leg to the finish line, his father held him up every step of the way! The stadium erupted with noise as fans cheered a father coming to his son's rescue!

When a father is absent in the life of his child, he loses the opportunity to be his child's hero, and the opportunity to rescue his child when he or she is in trouble.

We have young men out here today hooked on cocaine…heroin… and oxycodone…but where are their fathers to rescue them?

We have young women out here today trapped in relationships where they are being beaten and abused…but where are their fathers to rescue them?

We have young men today trying to get out of that gang life and the gang members won't let them…but where are their fathers to rescue them?

We have young women getting snatched off the streets and thrown into sex trafficking…but where are their fathers to rescue them?

Where are the fathers? Where are the heroes?

Heroes "rescue" their children!

In **1 Samuel 30**, David and his men had been away with the Philistines. When they returned to the city of Ziklag where they had been living, they found that the city had been raided by the Amalekites and their families had been taken hostage. All their wives, sons, and daughters had become captives of the Amalekites. David and his men wept greatly and were depressed because their sons and daughters had been carried off. It was here that David did three things: He **"encouraged himself,"** he **"inquired of God,"** and he **"engaged the enemy."**

    a. If you're going to **rescue** your child, you must **"encourage"** yourself.

1 Samuel 30:6

"And David was greatly distressed; for the people spake of stoning him, because the soul of all the people was grieved, every man for his sons and for his daughters: **but David encouraged himself in the Lord his God."**

Sometimes the biggest mistake we make is not trusting in the Lord and leaning to our own understanding. David had taken his men and their families to live with the Philistines to evade Saul who was trying to kill David. Though the Philistines were **"Israel's enemy,"** David convinced them he had sided with them because of Saul's threat against his life. This would be a mistake which would come back to haunt David. This mistake put David in the unenviable position of being responsible for the tragic events that had taken place. Being the leader made him responsible for putting the wives and children of he and his men in the position they were in.

It was at this point that David had to encourage himself in the Lord. David had to have the right frame of mind before attempting to rescue the wives and children taken into captivity. David didn't give up and David didn't give in even though things looked bad, and his own men were threatening to come against him. Rescuing our children is not an easy task, and there will be days filled with discouragement, but don't quit. Fight the good fight of faith, run the race with patience, endure to the end, **and encourage yourself in the Lord**.

As men, we often make mistakes that can have a negative impact on our children. Sometimes it's not being there when children need us. When we are not around, it often leaves our children **vulnerable** to the attack of the enemy. **Vulnerable** to the temptation of drugs, the lure of premarital sex, the influence of the wrong people, their own lack of self-control and poor judgment, and **vulnerable** to the ways of this world. When our children fall prey to these things, we can become extremely discouraged.

> b. If you're going to rescue your child, you must **"inquire"** of God.

1 Samuel 30:7-8

"Then David said to Abiathar the priest, Ahimelech's son, "Please bring the ephod here to me." And Abiathar brought the ephod to David. 8 So David inquired of the LORD, saying, "Shall I pursue this troop? Shall I overtake them?" And He answered him, "Pursue, for you shall surely overtake them and without fail recover all."

After David "encouraged himself," David sought guidance from the Lord. David "inquired of the Lord!" David had the ephod brought to him.

The ephod was part of the priestly garment worn when the priest went to the golden altars in prayer.

Rescuing our children from whatever is holding them captive is too great of a task for us to try to accomplish on our own. It is going to take divine guidance from God for us to know how to proceed. As men of God, we must understand what is at stake. The lives and destinies of our children hang in the balance. This is not a time to be filled with pride and arrogance. This is a time to humble ourselves, put our trust in the Lord, and depend on Him to give us the answers, and show us the way. It's through prayer and God's Word that we receive divine direction.

> **Prayer:**
>
> **Isaiah 65:24 (KJV)** *"And it shall come to pass, that before they call, I will answer; and while they are yet speaking, I will hear."*
>
> **Matthew 7:7-8 (KJV)** *"Ask, and it shall be given you; seek, and ye shall Find; knock, and it shall be opened unto you: For everyone that asketh receiveth; and he that seeketh Findeth; and to him that knocketh it shall be opened."*

The Word of God:

Psalm 119:105 (KJV) *"Thy word is a lamp unto my feet, and a light unto my path."*

The surest way for a man to gain victory in rescuing his child is by seeking the direction from God. God is all knowing, and He can always lead you in the right course of action no matter what we are trying to accomplish. We must learn to spend time in the Word of God, and in prayer. Lastly, we must put our utter confidence and trust in Him!

Proverbs 3:5-6 (KJV) *"Trust in the Lord with all thine heart; and lean not unto thine own understanding. In all thy ways acknowledge him, and he shall direct thy paths."*

   c. If you're going to rescue your child, you must "engage" the enemy.

In 2011, a movie was released entitled **Courageous** {1}. It was about four police officers dealing with tragedies, struggles, and faith in God. In the beginning of the movie, a man is at a gas station pumping gas into his truck. As he finishes pumping gas, he starts his truck preparing to pull off. He realizes that his windshield is dirty, so he exits the truck to clean his windshield while leaving the truck running and the driver's door open.

When he realizes that there is no window-washing solution at the bay where he is, he walks over to another bay. Suddenly, a man jumps in his vehicle, gets behind the wheel, closes the door and takes off.

Realizing what just happened, the owner runs to the driver's side of the truck holding on to the window and fighting the carjacker. The owner is fighting with all his might to gain control of his vehicle. Punches are thrown; the steering wheel is grabbed, as the truck begins weaving out of control.

Finally, the owner is thrown from the side of the truck and the truck crashes into a tree. The airbags inflate and the dazed carjacker flees the scene in another truck that was following him that was part of the attempted carjacking.

A passersby stopped to try and help the owner but the only thing the owner is concerned with is getting to the truck. When he finally opens the back door of the truck, there is a baby in a car seat crying. It's at this point that we realize what he was fighting for! It's at this point that we realize what was so important! It was at this point that we realized what he was willing to risk his life for!

He was fighting to rescue his child. He was willing to risk his own life by engaging the enemy to save his own child. In this case, all that mattered was achieving victory over the enemy. **Some victories you must fight for.**

1 Samuel 30:17-19 (NLT)

"David and his men rushed in among them and slaughtered them throughout that night and the entire next day until evening. None of the Amalekites escaped except four hundred young men who Fled on camels. David got back everything the Amalekites had taken, and he rescued his two wives. Nothing was missing: small or great, son or daughter, nor anything else that had been taken. David brought everything back."

After David **"encouraged himself,"** and after David **"inquired of the Lord,"** he and his men **"engaged the enemy."** David and his men located the place where the Amalekites were camped. The Amalekites were eating, drinking, dancing, and celebrating all they had taken. David and his men engage the enemy in what the Bible describes as a battle that lasted that night, the next day, and into the evening. But the good news is at the end of the battle. David and his men retrieved all the livestock, flocks, and herds that the Amalekites had taken, recovered all the women taken, **and rescued all the children.**

There is no way to rescue your child without **"engaging the enemy."** The **enemy** could be things that have a stronghold in your child's life like self-destructive behavior related to drugs or alcohol. The **enemy** could be some sexual or physically abusive behavior. The **enemy** could be people who are leading them down the wrong paths of life. The **enemy** could be their involvement in the occult or other forms of demonic activity. Whatever the **enemy** is, you must identify it, and engage it.

Engaging the enemy may mean having to confront your child about the enemy's attack in their life and then getting your children into counseling or treatment.

Engaging the enemy may mean humbling yourself and asking the child's forgiveness for the harm you have caused them. Remember, your child may have years of pain, pent up hurt, unforgiveness, and bitterness toward you for your absence in their life. It may take every bit of patience and going to any means necessary to win your child's love, trust, and forgiveness.

Engaging the enemy may mean the total onslaught of spiritual warfare including fervent prayer, turning your plate down and fasting, receiving direction from the Bible, God's Word, allowing the Holy Spirit to fill you and guide you, relying on and seeking God to pull down all strongholds in your child's life and in your life. Remember, God gives us the recipe for spiritual warfare in **2 Corinthians 10:4-6, and in Ephesians 6:10-18**.

Rescuing our children means doing whatever is needed, including engaging the enemy. The enemy has taken many of our children as hostages. The enemy has abducted many of our children, and we often don't know the effect the enemy has had on our children while we were apart from them.

There is a psychological response to abduction called **"Stockholm Syndrome,"** where the victim develops a loyalty to the abductor no matter the risk, danger, or harm to themselves. This loyalty to the abuser is often seen in cases of domestic violence, child abuse, and gang affiliation. Sometimes our children develop an emotional attachment to the thing or person who has them in bondage, causing them harm, and contributing to the child's already fragile negative self-image.

We must always be ready to counter the attack of the enemy over our children with love, patience, and words of affection and affirmation that build up our children and undermine the works of the enemy.

> **Proverbs 18:21 (KJV)** *"Death and life are in the power of the tongue: and they that love it shall eat the fruit thereof."*

Finally, remember that David and his men didn't get the victory immediately. It took them all night, all day, and into the next night before they were victorious. Victory doesn't always happen overnight, as a matter of fact, it seldom does. Your victory may not come immediately, because some victories take time.

In **Exodus 23**, God's people had already been delivered from Egyptian slavery and were on their way to the land God had promised them. God tells them that His angel will prepare a way for them by guiding them and protecting them. That God will destroy their enemies and drive out the Hivite, the Canaanite, and the Hittite before you. In verse 30 of this chapter, God tells them how He was going to do it.

> *"Little by little I will drive them out from before you, until you have increased, and you inherit the land."* **Exodus 23:30 (KJV)**

God says, "I'm not going to make it happen all at once, but I will make it happen, **'little by little.'**"

That's why you must be patient with your children. God will give you success and victory when it comes to your children, but sometimes He does it, **"little by little."** We don't know why He does it **"little by little"** instead of all at once, but God does. God says, "Be patient and faithful and,

Little by little you'll gain their trust

Little by little you'll earn their respect

Little by little you'll see their forgiveness

Little by little you'll see them change

Little by little you'll receive their love

Fathers, you do your part, and "little by little" you'll see God perform a miracle with you and your children.

Fathers, "Encourage yourself, inquire of the Lord, and engage the enemy."

Because that's what "heroes" do!

As a parent, there will come a day in your life when your child comes to you and tell you they are in trouble. The trouble may be something minor (but major in their eyes), or the trouble may have ramifications that could alter their entire future and destiny. In my case, it was the latter. It was when I received a call from one of my children stating that he was facing a disciplinary hearing that could possibly lead to his expulsion from the university. It stemmed from an altercation he and a friend had with another student. Initially, I was furious. Thinking my child could find himself in a situation like that, knowing my criminal justice background, all the stories I had told him about this kind of behavior, and the fact that my child had worked for two summers at the local police department, it made no sense. Did I forget to mention that I got myself into a similar situation when I was in college? I think that's why my mother used to always say, "I can't wait for you to have kids" (smile).

After my memory, and my mother's words had convicted me of my past, I calmed down. I decided that my wife and I would drive from Cleveland, Ohio — ten hours to where our child went to school to support him in this matter.

Having seen hundreds of young people who had appeared in court without a parent to show support or concern, there was no way that I was going to allow my child to face this by himself. His father was going to be there with him. I did not look forward to the ten-hour drive, most of which was through the winding hills and mountains of West Virginia and Virginia, but my wife and I made the trek and was there for the hearing.

We prayed before the hearing that God would touch the hearts of those who would make the decision that would ultimately impact our child's future. We prayed during the hearing and after the hearing while we awaited their decision.

Several hours later, we received their decision. The counsel showed our child grace and mercy, and he was not suspended or expelled from the university.

Some may believe that if your child gets in trouble, it's on them to either get out of it, or to face the consequences by themselves. I believe it's a father's (parent) responsibility to come to the aid and rescue of his child…**because that's what "heroes" do!**

There may come a time when the only person who can rescue a child, reach them and save them is their father.

In 1989, Steven Spielberg directed an epic film co-written by George Lucas titled **Indiana Jones and the Last Crusade** {2}. The movie was a sequel to the box office hit, **Raiders of the Lost Ark,** starring Harrison Ford as Indiana Jones. In this sequel, Indiana Jones and his father Henry, played by Sean Connery, are on a quest to find the Holy Grail, the cup Jesus drank from at the last supper prior to His crucifixion.

Fast forward to the end, Indiana is hanging on for dear life from the cavern with his father holding on to one of his hands trying to save him. Indiana's other hand is almost in reach of the grail which is on the opposite ledge. Another person who was just in the same situation fell to their death trying to grab on to the Holy Grail.

Indiana is so obsessed with getting the grail he is not even considering the danger he is in. His father, doing all he can to save him says **"Junior, give me your other hand I can't hold on."** Indiana only focusing on the grail says, **"I can get it, I can almost reach it dad."** Then his father says to him in a calm, almost surreal tone, **"Indiana, Indiana, let it go."** It's at this point Indiana looks his father in the face, comes to his senses, and gives his father his other hand and is pulled up to safety. It was only when his loving father spoke those words to him that he surrendered to his father's will and let him save him.

> **Fathers need to be there to rescue their children often from themselves.**

Heroes "rescue" their children.

~ Journal ~

Chapter 7

HEROES 'RESTORE' THEIR CHILDREN

We must remember when we are dealing with children that they have not lived as long as we have lived. They have not experienced the things we have experienced, and they have not learned the lessons we have learned.

Just like us, our children are prone to making mistakes, and sometimes their mistakes cause a strain in our relationship with them. But they are our children, and as fathers, we must temper justice with mercy, and discipline with compassion, and that means as **heroes we need to always seek to "restore our children to a right relationship with us."**

My all-time favorite story in the Bible is the parable of the Prodigal Son found in the Gospel of Luke, chapter 15, and verses 11-24.

The story of the **"Prodigal Son"** told by Jesus to the self-righteous leaders of his time was to demonstrate the love God has for a sinful man who has strayed away from God. But I believe that this story has practical principles we can apply when it comes to restoring our relationship with a child who may have strayed.

In the story, the younger of two sons demands that his father give him his inheritance while the father is still alive (what an insulting request from a child to his parents). The father complies with his son's request and, shortly thereafter, the son leaves home and travels to a distant land and wastes all his inheritance on partying and prostitutes.

Not long after, a famine sweeps the land, and the son becomes destitute. The only work he could find was feeding pigs, which was considered one of the most disgraceful things a person of his culture could do. To make matters worse, the son was so hungry that he desired to eat the same things the pigs ate.

It was at that moment that he came to his senses, realized the error of his ways, and decided to return to his father's home, ask him for forgiveness, and for a job as a servant. As he approached the house, his father saw him from a great distance.

It is at this point in the story that I want to bring out three things the father did to restore his son; **"initiate," demonstrate," and "celebrate."**

> a. If you want to restore your child, *"initiate His restoration."*
>
> **Luke 15:20 (NIV)**
>
> *"So he got up and went to his father. "But while he was still a long way off, his father saw him and was filled with compassion for him; he ran to his son, threw his arms around him and kissed him."*

The father in this story didn't wait for his son to reach him, he ran to his son. Can you see this beautiful picture of a father, who desired for his son's return so much that when he caught a glimpse of him from afar, he couldn't wait for his son to come to him, but he had to run to his son?

Godly fathers initiate the restoration of their child. They run to their child, they embrace their child, they kiss their child. The father's compassion for his child was shown by the affection he showed his child.

This is a beautiful picture of what God, our Father, did for us. He didn't wait for us to come to Him (which we couldn't). He came to us in the person of His son Jesus Christ, and then showed His compassion for us through Jesus dying on a cross for our sins. Just like our Heavenly Father initiated our restoration, we as fathers, and "heroes," need to initiate the move toward our child's restoration.

>b. If you want to restore your child **"demonstrate his restoration."**
>
>**Luke 15:22 (NLT)**
>
>*"But his father said to the servants, 'Quick! Bring the Finest robe in the house and put it on him. Get a ring for his Finger, and sandals for his feet.'"*

After the father "initiates the restoration" toward his son, the next thing he does is "demonstrate the restoration" by giving him a robe, a ring, and some sandals. When the child returned home, he was bankrupt, monetarily, morally, and spiritually. Having worked in the pig pen, it is probably reasonable to assume his clothes were worn out, filthy, and smelly. The first thing the father did was to cover his son's filthy appearance with the finest robe in the house. Next, he put a ring on his finger. In ancient times, the ring was a signet ring, which was used to officially give personal authority to a document in lieu of a signature. Lastly, he gave him sandals for his feet. The significance there was that only a family member could wear sandals inside the master's house. All the father's actions were to demonstrate to the son and all others that his son had been fully restored with all the rights and privileges that he had before he left. The father withheld nothing from his son.

As fathers and "heroes," we must show our child and the world that we have restored our child, no matter what he or she has done.

This is not a time to throw in their face what they did, it is a time to demonstrate our love and desire to have them back. Not once did the father say, "I told you so," or "This is the last time I put up with your mess," or "The next time you are on your own," or "You are no longer my child."

Again, this is a picture of what our Heavenly Father has done for His children. He robes us with His righteousness covering up the filth of our sins ("I am overwhelmed with joy in the Lord my God! For He has dressed me with the clothing of salvation and draped me in a robe of righteousness.") **Isaiah 61:10a (NLT)**, and He restores us as His children with all rights and privileges through Jesus Christ, ("But as many as received him (Jesus), to them gave the power to become the sons of God, even to them that believe on his name:") **John 1:12 (KJV)**.

> c. If you want to restore your child *"celebrate his restoration."*
>
> **Luke 15:23-24 (NIV)**
>
> *"Bring the fattened calf and kill it. Let's have a feast and celebrate. For this son of mine was dead and is alive again; he was lost and is found.' So they began to celebrate."*

After he **"initiates"** and **"demonstrates"** his child's restoration, the father **"celebrates"** his child's restoration. The father had a party for his son upon his return. This was a festive occasion for the father, the family, and the restored son.

There was a feast, there was music, and there was dancing according to the rest of the story. Restoration is a time of celebration. It is a time to celebrate the restoring of relationships. It is a time to celebrate the future without dwelling on the past. It is a time of thanksgiving and gratitude. It's a time of celebration of the healing that takes place in a family between a parent and their child because of the power of restoration.

Heaven celebrates every time someone who was lost in sin is restored into God's family through a relationship with Jesus Christ.

> **Luke 15:7** *"I say unto you, that likewise joy shall be in heaven over one sinner that repenteth, more than over ninety and nine just persons, which need no repentance."*

> **Luke 15:10** *"Likewise, I say unto you, there is joy in the presence of the angels of God over one sinner that repenteth."*

As I stated earlier, David was the greatest king in the history of Israel, but he fell short when it came to parenting his children. The story of David and his children teaches us some valuable lessons when it comes to fathers raising their children.

Let me give you a quick synopsis of some of the events that took place with David and his children and the impact that these events had. In later chapters, we will look at other aspects of David's relationship with his children.

David had many wives, so not all his children had the same mother. That had an impact on how his children viewed and treated one another. This is not surprising since we have seen this before in the Bible.

Look at Isaac and Ishmael's dysfunctional relationship because of them having different mothers. Look at Joseph's dysfunctional relationships with most of his brothers, which was rooted in the fact that his siblings were the result of four different women. The dynamics of blended families can have their difficulties and challenges. David's blended family was no different.

This story concerning David and his children is what can happen when a father fails to restore their child.

The problem began when the oldest son Amnon had lustful desires for his half-sister Tamar. He didn't look at her as his sister, he looked at her in a purely sexual fashion, though in his mind it was love. If she had been his sister from the same mother, he might not have allowed his lust to overwhelm him.

As the story continues, Amnon rapes his half-sister Tamar, disregarding her pleas for him not to, then discards her like trash. Tamar is left devastated, but we will look further into this later.

David was furious when he found out what happened, but he did nothing. Absalom, David's second son, and the brother of Tamar, is enraged by what his half-brother did to his sister from the same mother Tamar. Absalom eventually avenges his sister Tamar by killing Amnon. David mourns Amnon's death and Absalom flees in fear, and though David misses Absalom, he does nothing to restore his son.

Absalom stayed away from David and his home for three years. At the urging of David's advisor Joab, David allowed Absalom to return from Geshur to Jerusalem, but look what **2 Samuel 14:23-24, 28 says**,

> *"Then Joab went to Geshur and brought Absalom back to Jerusalem. 24 But the king said, "He must go to his own house; he must not see my face." So Absalom went to his own house and did not see the face of the king.... 28 Absalom lived two years in Jerusalem without seeing the king's face."* **(NIV)**

At this point, five years had gone by, and David did nothing to restore his son Absalom. Unlike the father in the prodigal son, David made no effort to initiate restoration. He did nothing privately to demonstrate restoration, and he does nothing publicly to celebrate that restoration with Absalom has taken place.

This says something about the condition of David's heart toward his son Absalom. One could surmise that there was still unforgiveness in David's heart toward his son. This is the same David who in **Psalm**

51:10 cried out to God, *"Create in me a clean heart, O God; and renew a right spirit within me."* **(KJV)**

There may also have been other reasons that David did not restore Absalom, reasons that may have been legitimate, including teaching Absalom humility by not allowing him in the royal court for his actions. But the result of not restoring Absalom would've been devastating for David.

Absalom would become rebellious and vindictive toward his father. He would go out of his way to cause David pain and humiliation. Absalom, in a calculated move, stole the hearts of King David's people.

To humiliate his father, Absalom took his father's concubines and slept with them. Then, Absalom made an all-out assault to overthrow his father's reign as king, by taking his throne from him, causing his father to flee Jerusalem for his life. In the end, Absalom gathered his troops against David's warriors but Absalom was killed in battle. David's heart was crushed at the death of his son.

Even though God had decreed that David's household would be full of turmoil because of what David did to Uriah, the husband of Bathsheba, this tragic story of David and Absalom may have been avoided if David would have reconciled with Absalom and restored his son.

Fathers, when it comes to our children who we have rescued out of their destructive circumstances, we need to put aside our anger, our hurt feelings, our disappointments, and our self-righteous pride, and restore our children in love, compassion, and gentleness, understanding that more important than our bruised ego is our child.

When a father refuses or fails to restore his child, nothing good can ever come out of it. The Apostle Paul teaches us all the importance of the principle of restoration.

Galatians 6:1 *"Brothers, if someone is caught in a sin, you who are spiritual should restore him gently. But watch yourself, or you also may be tempted."* **ESV**

Restoring one's child should always be a priority in a father's life… **Because that's what heroes do…**

Heroes "restore" their children.

~ Journal ~

Chapter 8

"WHAT EVERY SON NEEDS FROM A FATHER"

How does a boy learn what it is to be a man? Harvard psychologist Samuel Osherson writes: *"What does it mean to be male? If the father is not there to provide a confident, rich model of manhood, then the boy is left in a vulnerable position....this solution places great pressure on the growing son....we often misidentify with our fathers, crippling our identities as men."* {1}
(Finding our Fathers - NY: Fawcett/Columbine 1986, pg.6)

There is a difference between being a **"male"** and being a **"man."** A **"male"** is simply the product of the proper chromosomes brought together when the female egg is fertilized by the male sperm and results in the conception of a male child. **Being a "male" speaks to "gender." Being a "man" speaks to "growth."**

A **"man"** is the product of what a **"male"** grows into by being imparted with *character, integrity, strength, courage, perseverance, maturity, knowledge, wisdom, Godly fear, reverence, and a manly persona.*

This impartation should be made by the father of this male. In some cases when the father is not in the male's life then these characteristics are imparted by another significant man in the male's life.

The bottom line is this though: "males" are born, but "men" are made!

When a father has been out of his son's life for a period, often there is a process of molding that must take place. It is not enough to only **"rescue"** your son. It is not enough to only **"restore"** your son. But there will often come a time when you will have to invest in the process of **"molding"** your son.

Because of the father's absence in the son's life, there is no telling what or who has begun to influence the son, and in what way. Your son may have developed habits dangerous to his well-being. Your son may have embraced core values that may be counter to the values God wants us to embrace. Your son may be lacking those things that are needed to take him from just being a male to being a man.

It is at this stage that the father must reinvest into the child's life so that molding can take place. It is what David does with Solomon as he is approaching death.

1 Kings 2:1-3 (David & Solomon)

King David has reached a ripe old age, and he is now approaching death. David has had an illustrious career. David went from a sheepherder to the king of Israel. He was catapulted from obscurity to notoriety when he defeated the Philistine champion Goliath.

He had many victories and successes in his life, but all his success and victories later in life came at a cost to his family. His daughter was raped by his son. His other son killed that son. That son tried to take over his kingdom and was eventually killed. Another son attempted to take the kingdom as David was nearing death.

Much of what happened in the life of David's family had to do with David so busy being king, that he failed to handle his responsibility as father. To make some investment in one of his children, David began the process of attempting to **"mold"** his son Solomon. Whenever you spend an extended period out of your son's life, there is a necessity for a father to put his molding imprint in that child's life. **"Molding"** is necessary!

David attempts to instill three things in his son Solomon in this **"molding"** process. David presents to his son a strategy for success that includes *inward confidence, outward character, and upward commitment!*

A. Inward confidence — *"Be strong"*

1 Kings 2:1-2a *"As David's time to die drew near, he charged Solomon his son, saying, 2 "I am going the way of all the earth. Be strong, therefore"* **(NASB)**

It is a father's responsibility to instill strength and confidence in his son. David tells Solomon to be strong. The word "strong" here is not speaking about physical strength, but strength of character, conviction, and inner strength. The strength to stand behind your convictions and your beliefs, the strength to stand behind your word, your vows, and your promises, while maintaining the strength not to waiver in adversity.

The Hebrew word for **"strong"** is the same word used for **"courage."**

2 Samuel 10:12 says,

"Be of good courage, and let us play the men for our people, and for the cities of our God: and the Lord do that which seemeth him good." **(ASV)**

The word **"courage"** in the Hebrew is **"chazaq."** It means to **"fasten upon,"** or **"to seize."** It denotes bravery, or one who is valiant. The phrase *"let us play the men"* is also translated, *"let us fight bravely."*

A father's responsibility is to instill inner strength, courage, and bravery into his son. If a father does not pour these qualities into his son, then his son may acquire other characteristics like timidity, bashfulness, or cowardice. He may not only experience fear, but he may wind up being ruled by fear.

In the movie **The Wizard of Oz**, the cowardly lion gives a speech about the one thing he does not have and that is *courage*. Listen to what he says;

"Courage! What makes a king out of a slave? Courage! What makes the flag on the mast to wave? Courage! What makes the elephant charge his tusk in the misty mist, or the dusky dusk? Courage! What makes the muskrat guard his musk? Courage! What makes the sphinx the seventh wonder? Courage! What makes the dawn come up like thunder? Courage! What makes the Hottentot so hot? What puts the "ape" in apricot? What have they got that I ain't got?" {2}

Dorothy, Scarecrow, and the Tin Man respond, *"Courage!"* The Cowardly Lion says, *"You can say that again! Huhh!"* Like David, we must teach our sons to be strong, brave, and have courage. A father must inspire that strength that produces an inner confidence in his son.

Fathers guide their sons into the courage that comes with manhood.

Indian Rites of Passage:

There is a legend of the Cherokee Indian youth's rite of passage. The father blindfolds his son and takes him into the forest late at night. He has his son sit on a tree stump the whole night without taking off the blind fold. He tells his son that he is leaving but that the son must sit there the entire night until the rays of the sun shine through the blindfold. He tells his son that he cannot cry out for help to anyone, and he must sit there all by himself. Once he survives the night, he is a MAN. Throughout the night, the boy is terrified. He hears all kinds of noises. He hears the owls hooting, he hears the wolves howling, he hears the mountain lions roaring, he hears snakes rattling. He is scared but remains seated on the stump. When the morning comes and he sees the sun rays through the blindfold, he takes it off. It's then he realizes that all night long, his father was there standing over him with his bow drawn. His father never left him but was there with him to lead him into manhood. Fathers must be around to lead their sons to manhood and courage.

B. Outward Character — *"show yourself a man"*

1 Kings 2:2b *"and show yourself a man."* **(NASB)**

Fathers must implant a sense of character into their sons that will be visible in their actions. A father must instill those qualities in his son that undoubtedly affirms his identity as a man, not just a male. It's about growth to manhood, not just male gender. Qualities like honesty, loyalty, faithfulness, trustworthiness, dependability, honor, and respect.

The phrase *"shew thyself a man,"* means for a male to present a manly persona, it means presenting a masculine stature of oneself. It means that a son should exhibit manly behavior and personality. That behavior and personality is rooted and reflective of manly character and integrity. It personifies growth and maturity that is a result of growth and not just gender. It's a maleness that is manly and mature.

I said manly, not chauvinistic. Over the years many men have interpreted being manly as being chauvinist. They believed being a man means showing dominance and superiority over our female counterparts. Treating them as less than, inferior, weak, unworthy, and a doormat to men. And when sons see their fathers treating their mothers and other women that way, they continue to perpetuate that mindset and behavior.

Manly does not mean brutish, overbearing, intimidating, bullying, or any behavior that demeans a woman or devalues a woman. It is essential that fathers portray an accurate depiction of manliness because that is something a woman cannot do. It takes a man to show a boy how to be a man, what manhood looks like.

A woman can teach a male child many wonderful and essential things in life. She can teach him to be sensitive. She can teach him to be thoughtful. She can teach him to be courteous.

A woman can do an excellent job of raising a male, and many women have done an excellent job of doing that and I congratulate them for it. But she cannot teach him the essence of being a man. It takes a man to impart manliness into a male child.

The same is true with a man and his female child. He can teach her integrity and character. He can teach her the strength of conviction and belief. He can teach her things to help her to grow educationally and spiritually. But he can't teach her to be a woman. It takes a woman to impart woman-ness into a female child.

Both of my daughters are accomplished beautiful women who I am proud of, but it wasn't me that molded them into the women they are. It was my wife, their mother, who did a phenomenal job of turning our little girls into the women they are today. My wife gets the credit for that, not me.

Just like it takes a woman to impart femininity into her daughter it takes a man to impart masculinity into his son. And though the world we live in may disagree, it's okay for a woman to exhibit femininity and a man to exhibit masculinity.

A man possesses a manner of maturity!

The Apostle Paul said in **1 Corinthians 13:11** *"When I was a child, I spake as a child, I understood as a child, I thought as a child: but when I became a man, I put away childish things."* **(KJV)**

Real men grow up! They grow up in their thinking. They grow up in their actions. They reflect a maturity that can be seen outwardly. Jesus' life was a life of maturity!

Luke 2:40 *"And the child grew, and waxed strong in spirit, filled with wisdom: and the grace of God was upon him."* **(KJV)**

Luke 2:52 *"And Jesus increased in wisdom and stature, and in favour with God and man."* **(KJV)**

David is telling Solomon, **"You are no longer a boy, display that inward character, and show that you are a man."**

C. Upward Commitment — *"Keep the charge of the Lord your God"*

First, David explains to Solomon the authority of **inward courage,** *"be strong."* Next, David tells Solomon the gravity of outward **character,** *"and show yourself a man."* Lastly, David reveals the necessity of **upward commitment,** *"Keep the charge of the Lord your God."*

> **1 Kings 2:3** *"Keep the charge of the LORD your God, to walk in His ways, to keep His statutes, His commandments, His ordinances, and His testimonies, according to what is written in the Law of Moses, that you may succeed in all that you do and wherever you turn,"* **(NASB)**

A man with an "upward commitment" possesses a spirit of submission to the Will of God and the Word of God.

David continues his charge to Solomon on manhood by telling him to come under subjection to God!

David tells Solomon to,

"Keep God's charge"

"Walk in God's way, keep God's statutes, commands, judgments, and testimonies."

In other words, David is saying to his son Solomon, **"Do what God tells you to do!'**

You may be asking, "How do I know the charge of God and the ways of God?" The answer is simple, they may be found in God's statutes, commands, judgments, and testimonies, another word, in the Word of God, the Scriptures, the Bible.

A man with an **"upward commitment"** does what God says, no matter how discomforting, no matter how challenging, no matter how much it goes against what he wants. A man with an "upward commitment" submits himself unto God! David says, "If a man does that, he will "succeed in all that you do and wherever you turn."

In my walk with God, I have learned a lot of things, some out of my willingness to obey, some out of consequences for not obeying. But these two things I am sure of. God rewards faithfulness and obedience to His Word. When a man is faithful and obedient to God's Word, blessings will follow that man (or that woman).

Saul, the king before David, lost his kingdom, the overshadowing power of the Holy Spirit, and the favor of God because of his disobedience toward God and God's commands. David, in turn would inherit the kingdom, would be endowed by the Holy Spirit, and experience God's favor all through his life. He had a heart for God, and for the most part, put God first. He was what the scriptures declared, "a man after God's own heart."

Sons need their fathers to instill in them, inward courage (strength), outward character (integrity), and upward commitment (obedience to God.)

When fathers instill those things into their sons, then they will see their sons transformed from boys to men, from male hood to manhood.

"Sons will become:

> Men who provide the **spiritual leadership** for his family,
> Men who provide the **love** a wife needs,
> Men who provide the **nurture** his children require,
> Men who provide the **needs and protection** his household depends on,

- ➤ Men who provide the **godly example** for his family,
- ➤ Men who provide **leadership** in their community,
- ➤ Men who provide the **character and influence** to be change agents the world so desperately needs."

The world needs fathers who will "man up" and show their sons what it is to be a man. We need "real fathers, real men."

~ Journal ~

Chapter 9

"DADDY'S LITTLE GIRL"

**Someone wrote that a father is
"A son's first hero and a daughter's first love"**

Just like a father should be his son's first hero, a father should be his daughter's first love. A daughter's idea of what a loving relationship looks like with a person of the opposite sex should come from her father.

A daughter should see it in how her father treats her mother. A daughter should experience it in how her father treats her. Her father should be the picture of how a man should treat a woman. Through her father she should see how a woman is to be respected, honored, protected, provided for, and loved by watching her father. That becomes the standard for her.

Through daddies, daughters learn what a real man looks like and what a real husband looks like. Without a daddy in her life, a daughter is left to try to define a man and a husband on her own. Without a daddy's example of manhood, a daughter may get an incorrect definition of manhood from another man. As a daddy, we must not put the image making responsibility of manhood in the hands of someone else when it comes to our daughters.

For many daughters, when a father and his love is absent from their life, they experience what is called the "father wound." Brya Hanan is a licensed marriage and family therapist, and certified family trauma specialist. In an article dated June 2, 2021, entitled *"Healing the Father Wound,"* Brya Hanan gives this definition of the "Father Wound," {1}

> *"The father wound is all about experiencing grief and loss. It is about feeling love, but instead feeling absence. It's the absence of love that makes the wound so profound. The absence of love doesn't just come from physical or emotional absence either."*

The father wound is directly connected to the father's absence, but it is not just about the father being physically absent. When a father is present in their daughter's life but emotionally withdrawn, or emotionally abusive, negative, or overly critical, the results are often emotionally wounded daughters.

Wounded daughters often experience painful and lasting effects from their wounds, such as:

- Negative self-image
- Anger, anxiety, depression
- Boundary issues (too inflexible or too loose)
- Relationship issues
    - ◊ Consistently in and out of relationships
    - ◊ Staying in dysfunctional or abusive relationships
    - ◊ Sexual encounters for the purpose of relieving pain
- Eating Disorders
- Weight-gain/weight-loss cycle
- Alcohol and substance abuse as a way to cope with and escape their hurt

Some believe that these issues are a result of a **father hunger** *caused by the father wound,* that hunger to fill the hollow and empty place in the heart and soul caused by the absence of a father's love. **Father wounds lead to father hunger.**

The bottom line is: "Daddy's little girl needs daddy's love."

A note to fathers: *"Your daughters are just as important as your sons."*

Society has placed a higher emphasis on fathers and sons. Fathers look to sons to carry on their last name. Fathers often live vicariously through their sons (sports). Fathers often put more of a priority on their son's interests than their daughter's. I hate to admit it, but in my youth as a father, I made the same mistake.

My son loved playing football and basketball like I did so I put an emphasis on attending his games and rooting him on. My daughter played in the school orchestra. I was nowhere near as supportive in attending her concerts and her desire in playing an instrument as I was in being at one of his football or basketball games. My daughter eventually lost interest in playing her instrument, and to this day, I wonder how much of it had to do with her father's lack of interest and support.

What message did I send to my daughter? That what was important to her wasn't important to me? That her brother's interests were more important to me than her interests? To this day, it is still one of my biggest regrets. I wish in life we had "do overs" because it would be on the top of my list.

By the time my second daughter was growing up, I had learned my lesson. When she was in elementary school, the school put on a "father-daughter dance." It was on a Friday night and there was probably some sporting event I could have been home watching, but the dance was important to her, so I took her to the dance.

When we arrived at the dance, she ran around with all the other little girls in their party dresses. She was laughing and dancing and having so much fun that it was worth me getting out of selfish daddy mode and doing something that brought her so much joy.

I learned that a father must be there for his daughter just as much as he was there for his son. **Daughters need their daddy…daughters need their daddy…daughters need their daddy.**

Nelson DeMille wrote a novel that was made into a movie entitled **The General's Daughter, which I referenced earlier in this book** {2}. The movie revolves around a female captain in the military named Elisabeth Campbell, a psychological operations officer, who is found dead and tied by her hands and feet to stakes. Elisabeth is the daughter of Lieutenant General "Fighting Joe" Campbell, who is about to leave the military to seek a career in politics.

John Travolta plays the role of Chief Warrant Officer Paul Brenner, who is sent to investigate the murder. As he and his partner navigate their way through lies and deceit, they learn that seven years earlier, Elisabeth, who was a cadet at West Point, was savagely tied to the ground and raped by a group of jealous male cadets. When her father, the general, learned what happened, he immediately flew to West Point, only to be greeted by a high-ranking official who presumably offered him another star on his shoulder, and advancement in his career if he would not pursue any actions that would bring shame to the academy.

When "Fighting Joe" goes to the hospital to see his beaten and raped daughter lying in a hospital bed, he tells her it would be better to just forget what had happen and act like nothing ever occurred. As he says this to her, you can see a tear roll down her cheek and the pain in her face as her father, the man who was supposed to be her protector and defender, betrays her for the advancement of his career.

In a time when she needed her father the most, to provide her comfort and love, and relief from her pain and hurt from the abuse she had suffered, he failed to give her what she needed. She spent the rest of her life until her dying moment trying to embarrass her father through a multitude of sexual affairs with soldiers under her command to make him feel the pain inside her because of his betrayal of her for the advancement of his career. **When she needed her daddy, he wasn't there.**

Some of you may say, "Well that was just a novel, that was nothing more than a movie." In real life, a father wouldn't respond that way if something like that happened to his daughter.

There is no way in the world a father would not come to his daughter's defense. No way would a father not be there emotionally for his daughter under those circumstances.

If you go back through the history of the Bible, you will see a similar situation occur with a somewhat similar outcome.

In **2 Samuel chapter 13** there is a real-life story about King David and a daughter of his named Tamar. In that story, Tamar has a half-brother named Amnon who has some irregular sexual feelings for his half-sister Tamar. Amnon thinks his feelings for Tamar are legitimate feelings of love, but his feelings are illegitimate feelings of lust.

> **"You can't always trust your feelings. Your feelings may tell you one thing when the truth says something else."**

With the help of a cousin, Amnon devises a plan where he pretends to be sick so he can be alone with Tamar. Once they're alone, he forces himself on her and rapes her. Here is how the Bible describes this event.

> *"Then Amnon said to Tamar, "Bring the food here into my bedroom so I may eat from your hand." And Tamar took the bread she had prepared and brought it to her brother Amnon in his bedroom. 11 But when she took it to him to eat, he grabbed her and said, "Come to bed with me, my sister." 12 "Don't, my brother!" she said to him. "Don't*

force me. Such a thing should not be done in Israel! Don't do this wicked thing. 13 What about me? Where could I get rid of my disgrace? And what about you? You would be like one of the wicked fools in Israel. Please speak to the king; he will not keep me from being married to you." 14 But he refused to listen to her, and since he was stronger than she, he raped her. 15 Then Amnon hated her with intense hatred. In fact, he hated her more than he had loved her. Amnon said to her, "Get up and get out!" 16 "No!" she said to him. "Sending me away would be a greater wrong than what you have already done to me." But he refused to listen to her. 17 He called his personal servant and said, "Get this woman out of here and bolt the door after her." 18 So his servant put her out and bolted the door after her." **2 Samuel 13:10-18b (NIV)**

The story goes on to say that both her other brother Absalom, and her father David found out what Amnon did to Tamar. We are told that Absalom in essence tells Tamar to keep what happened to herself and not worry about it since Amnon was her brother.

What an insensitive thing to say to your sister who has just been raped by her half-brother. **Secrets.** One of the big downfalls in many of our families is the secrets we keep. I've heard it said that we are just as sick as our secrets, and that goes for families also.

> **"The only way people and families can find healing is to confront and address the hidden issues in the family."**

But it gets worse. The Bible says that when David finds out what happens, he is furious but there is no record that David ever dealt with Amnon for what he did to Tamar. There is nothing saying he ever went to his daughter Tamar to comfort her in the time when she needed her daddy the most.

Could things be any worse for Tamar? Verse 20 answers that question.

"And Tamar lived in her brother Absalom's house, a desolate woman."

That word *desolate* means "alone, forsaken, without worth, a waste." It is said that a woman who was... *"shamed and raped in the culture of that day was as good as dead. Raped women stood little chance of ever being married and having a family."* {3} **(Preacher's outline and sermon Bible — commentary — 2 Samuel)**

Why didn't David come to Tamar in her time of crisis? Why did David comfort Tamar when she had been emotionally broken? Why didn't David defend Tamar and deal with the egregious abuse brought on her by her brother Amnon? Fathers can't prevent everything that happens to their children, but they can be there for their children when it happens.

Maybe David not responding to Tamar in her time of need was fear for his reputation if his own past sins were somehow exposed. Did David trade his loyalty to his daughter to keep his own reputation intact?

David is not the only father in scripture who failed his daughter. In **Genesis 19** when the wicked men of Sodom attempted to enter the house of a man named Lot to rape some guest he was entertaining, Lot offered his own daughters to the men of Sodom to protect his guest. How could a father offer up his daughters to be sexually abused? Lot's lack of value for his daughters says a lot about Lot.

Let me make it clear, **Psalms 127:3** says, *"Children are a gift from the Lord"* **(NLT)**. That means your daughters are God given, and God does not want you to forsake, neglect, or abandon your daughters. When you do that, you are telling God you are ungrateful for the gift He has given you. You are placing yourself in position to be cut off from future blessings.

The Lord has a special place in His heart for children, and just like Him, we ought to have a special place in our hearts for our children. As a matter of fact, the Lord says there are serious consequences for harming a child. The Lord said in **Matthew 18:6**, if someone offends one of His children, it would be better for that person to tie a large millstone around his neck and drown in the depths of the sea.

As fathers, we need to be like that man in the Bible named Jairus, who was one of the rulers of the synagogue. That means he had power, popularity, prestige, and pull.

None of that made a difference when his daughter was not well, some even said she was dead. His power couldn't raise her, his popularity couldn't raise her, his prestige couldn't raise her, and his pull couldn't raise her.

But he refused to give up when it came to his daughter. So, this man with all his power and prestige humbled himself for the sake of his daughter and went and found Jesus. When he found Jesus, he fell before him and begged Jesus to come see about his daughter so she might live. When Jesus reached Jairus' daughter, He took her by the hand and restored health and life into her body.

Power, prestige, popularity, and pull didn't matter to Jairus. The only thing that mattered to him was saving his daughter. Jairus teaches us fathers a powerful lesson. As fathers we, must be there for "Daddy's Little Girl."

We must be there to comfort them.

We must be there to protect them.

We must be there to defend them.

We must be there to save them.

We must be there to love them.

We must be there for Daddy's little girl because daughters need their daddies.

~ Journal ~

Chapter 10

"HE'S CALLED TO BE FATHER, NOT FRIEND"

One of the big problems in our society today is the redefining of the role of fathers. Society has increasingly attempted to diminish the role and the authority of the father when it comes to the training and disciplining of their children.

A father's discipline is no longer to include any corporal correction even though this expressly goes against what God says. This is what God says,

> *"Those who spare the rod of discipline hate their children. Those who love their children care enough to discipline them."* **Proverbs 13:24 (NLT2)**

> *"A youngster's heart is filled with foolishness, but physical discipline will drive it far away."* **Proverbs 22:15 (NLT2)**

> *"Don't fail to discipline your children. They won't die if you spank them. 14 Physical discipline may well save them from death."* **Proverbs 23:13-14 (NLT2)**

By no means am I suggesting the physical abuse of any child. I am just sharing what word of God clearly states regarding disciplining and correcting our children when they are young. God says that disciplining and correcting our children proves we love them. That discipline drives foolishness out of them which can lead to saving their life.

Society, with all its theories and studies would have us believe that it knows more about raising and training children than the God who created all life and who gives children to parents as a gift. Society says the Biblical correction should be replaced with punishments, time outs, and withholding things that our children have. Society also says that if a father corrects and disciplines a child the way the Bible says, then that father should face court actions, and the child should be removed from the father's authority.

As a result of that kind of thinking, we have children growing up who don't fear or respect adult authority. They don't feel that they must obey and honor their parents. They believe they can talk to their parents any way they want to and can use profanity and physical force against their parents.

Society has undermined a father's ability to raise a child as instructed by God. So even if the father is present in his child's life and not absent, his authority over his children has been compromised.

Society wants fathers to be their children's friends and not a parental figure. They want children and fathers to have a peer relationship with each other as any other friends would have. Men are called to be their children's parental figures, not their peer friends.

As seen in the scriptures I presented earlier, children need discipline, and if fathers fail to discipline their children, they fail their child.

Young Elephants and Old Elephants

There is an old story told about a wildlife sanctuary that was built to be a safe haven for animals from the jungles of Africa. There were all types of animals living in this sanctuary, with each species living in their own particular areas. The giraffes, lions, tigers, gorillas, and monkeys had their areas, and so on and so forth.

The elephants had their area but there was a problem. All the elephants were young males, and they were wild. They destroyed the sanctuary by fighting each other and creating havoc. Those young male elephants were out of control and the wildlife conservationists couldn't figure out how to get the young bull elephants under control.

Finally, news got to the conservationist that there were no older adult male elephants in the herd. It was the young elephants that were causing all the chaos. The reason there were no adult male elephants was because poachers had killed many of them for their ivory.

The conservationist flew in some adult male elephants and placed them in the herd. When the adult male elephants were placed into the midst of the chaos, they began flapping their ears, stomping their feet, raising their trunks, and making loud sounds.

Immediately after flapping their ears, stomping their feet, raising their trunks, and making loud sounds, the young male elephants calmed down and stopped all their destructive behavior.

As long as the young male elephants were calling the shots, you had a gang of elephants that were terrorizing the wildlife sanctuary. However, when the adult male elephants came on the scene, they demanded order and the young elephants got in their place.

We've got some teenage terrorists in our communities today who are undisciplined, out of control, and terrorizing the neighborhoods because there are no adult male elephants in the midst. We need some adult male elephants – real men, real fathers, who will flap their ears, stomp their feet, raise their trunks, and sound out the truth to calm down these young elephants we call our children.

Children, especially sons, need their father's discipline!

Allow me to give you several examples from the Word of God of what happens when discipline is ignored, and children go unchecked:

Eli and His Sons

Eli was a priest whose story can be found in the Book of 1 Samuel. The life of Eli is summarized in his profile in the Life Application Bible. Here's what it says:

> *"Eli was one Old Testament person with a very modern problem. The recognition and respect he earned in public did not extend to his handling of his private affairs. He may have been an excellent priest, but he was a poor parent. His sons brought him grief and ruin. He lacked two important qualities needed for effective parental discipline: firm resolve and corrective action."*

Eli had two sons, Hophni and Phinehas, who were priests, but they were wicked and corrupt. They were taking the choice meat that a person was offering to the Lord. They were taking portions of the Lord's offering, and they were involved in sexual immorality with women at the door of the tabernacle. The Bible says Eli's sons *"did not know the Lord."*

When Eli heard what his sons were doing, he spoke to them about it but that was all. He didn't remove them from their duties, he didn't bring them before the leaders, and he did nothing to discipline his sons.

As a result, the Lord told Eli that he was going to let Eli's family lineage die out, forever cutting them out of the line of priests because Eli failed to deal with the sins of his sons. The Lord further said that because Eli had honored his sons ahead of the Lord, as a sign of His judgment that both of Eli's sons would die on the same day.

The destiny of Eli's entire family would come to an end because Eli didn't discipline his sons.

Samuel and His Sons

Samuel was a judge, prophet, and priest who grew up assisting Eli the priest in the tabernacle until God had other work for him. When

Samuel reached old age, his sons, Joel and Abijah, who were judges, were not just in their dealings like their father. They took bribes, they were greedy for money, and they corrupted justice.

When the elders came to Samuel about his sons, there was nothing in the record that says Samuel took any corrective actions in disciplining his sons.

The actions of Samuel's sons led to the leaders demanding a king like the heathen nations as opposed to being ruled under the authority of God.

The whole way the nation would proceed from that moment forward was a direct result of the actions of Samuel's ungodly sons, and Samuel's inaction when it came to disciplining them.

David and His Sons

As you have seen, I've spent a lot of time reflecting on the mess that took place in David's household. To be honest, much of the tragedy that took place with David's children was self-inflicted. David took his servant Uriah's wife, slept with her, and plotted the death of Uriah. God told David through the Prophet Nathan that his household would be forever plagued with trouble. Add to the fact that David was so busy being king that being a father was not a priority for him.

> *"When your children are not your priority they become your problem."*

As I previously shared, when David learned that his oldest son raped his half-sister Tamar, David's daughter, David did nothing. David became furious, but he did nothing. David did not take any corrective actions against his son Amnon.

David's son Absalom took matters into his own hands and devised a scheme to kill his brother Amnon for raping his sister. Again, David did nothing to Absalom for killing his brother Amnon. This was another example where David failed to discipline a son.

Finally, Absalom attempted to overthrow his father David's kingdom and steal his throne. David found himself fleeing from Absalom because he had no respect for his father. Absalom would eventually die because of his tyranny against his father, but it was not at the hands of David. David is a prime example of a father who was not invested in his children, and who failed to discipline his children, leading to the unraveling of his family.

Eli failed to discipline his sons, eliminating his family from the priestly line. Samuel failed to discipline his sons and the nation rejected God as their leader. David failed to discipline his sons leading to the death of two of his sons and leaving his family in turmoil. That's what happens when you ignore what God tells you.

> **"As fathers, we don't just dole out discipline. We bring up our children in the ways that God has shown us in His Word."**

Maybe if Eli had disciplined his son, judgment would not have fallen on his family. Maybe if Samuel had disciplined his sons, the nation would not have replaced God with a king. Maybe if David had disciplined his sons, they both would not have been violently killed. Being a father is a grave responsibility and the consequences of failure can have generational ramifications.

Fathers are to help their children navigate this thing called life by giving them instruction and guidance. The instruction and guidance of a father helps their children avoid some of the pitfalls of life.

Dr. Tony Evans said this about fathers:

"Satellites are often used to show us where the enemy is located. They provide pictures and perspectives so that we are kept from ambushes and traps. They provide information critical for being victorious in war. Fathers are supposed to be like satellites, providing perspectives for their

kids in order to keep them from being ambushed in illegitimate relationships."

(Tony Evans Book of illustrations pg. 103) {1}

Here are some scriptures showing the parental duties fathers were to provide for their children:

Teach children:

"These words, which I am commanding you today, shall be on your heart. 7 "You shall teach them diligently to your sons and shall talk of them when you sit in your house and when you walk by the way and when you lie down and when you rise up." **Deuteronomy 6:6-7 (NASB)**

Train children: (initiate or discipline)

"Train up a child in the way he should go, Even when he is old he will not depart from it." **Proverbs 22:6 (NASB)**

Nurture children:

"Fathers, do not embitter your children, or they will become discouraged." **Colossians 3:21 (NIV)**

That's why fathers must be fathers in their children's lives and respected by their children and society.

~ Journal ~

Chapter 11

"A GENERATION THAT DID NOT KNOW GOD"

"And also, all that generation were gathered unto their fathers: and there arose another generation after them, which knew not the Lord, nor yet the works which he had done for Israel." **Judges 2:10 (Darby)**

In the mid to late 90's, a rash of mass shootings and killings took place in many high schools across this nation by young teenage males.

In **Extreme Evil: Kids Killing Kids**, Bob Larson profiled nine teenage boys who had committed these types of murders and came away with this finding:

"Of these nine young killers described above, four came from troubled homes. (And we have no way of knowing what went on behind the closed doors of the other Five; some of those families may have been equally dysfunctional.)

"One-third of the killers were taking prescription, mind altering drugs, and more than half of them were recreational drug users. None excelled academically, none was popular in mainstream campus culture, and none had a circle of morally and socially stable friends. All were either

> *without opposite sex relationships or had suffered the indignity of female rejection.*
>
> *"They were put down, put upon, teased, and bullied. Most importantly, there doesn't seem to be a single instance in which any of them were deeply spiritual, and none had parents who professed Christian faith as a dominant fact of family life.*
>
> *"In most cases, it was what these kid killers didn't have that characterizes them. They didn't have acceptance. They weren't well-liked, and no one seemed to sense their deep feeling of isolation and identity crisis. They weren't connected to other family or community members.*
>
> *"Several had brushes with Christianity, but not one of them confessed an active participation in church life. Whatever else they didn't have, they didn't have a strong faith in God."* **(Chapter 2, pgs. 30,31) {1}**

There is a generation of young people today that are violent and savage. All you must do is go on any social media site and you can find videos of teenage boys fighting in the streets, or packs of teenage girls fighting at shopping plazas and malls. It's as though they saw nothing wrong in what they were doing. It's as though it was a way of life to them.

They have grown up without any love in their heart for God and much less for their fellow man. They have embraced violence, sexual perversion, profanity, misogynistic language, and every type of base human behavior imaginable. They are prideful, materialistic, self-centered and selfish, thirsting for popularity and celebrity status, and have no respect for parents, the law, or the value of life.

The Bible speaks of this generation:

> *"There is a generation that curseth their father, and doth not bless their mother. There is a generation that are pure in their own eyes, and yet is not washed from their Filthiness. There is a generation, O how lofty are their eyes! and their eyelids are lifted up. There is a generation, whose*

teeth are as swords, and their jaw teeth as knives, to devour the poor from off the earth, and the needy from among men." **Proverbs 30:11-14, (KJV)**

I believe that many of our young people are this way because they have no relationship with Jesus Christ, nor God in their life. There was no father in their life who impressed upon them the importance of God in their life and living a godly life in accordance with the Word of God! This responsibility falls squarely on the man who God has called to be the spiritual head and leader of the family!

You may be asking the question, *"How is this related to the absence and presence of fathers?"* In ancient times, it was the responsibility of the father to give instructions to his children. Fathers were home with the family most of the time except during some military battle. Fathers were at home taking care of the land, dressing, or tilling it, planting vegetables and fruit bearing trees, and caring for the cattle and the sheep, digging wells, hunting, and fishing.

Most of the time when the father was in the fields doing all these things, his son would be with him learning from him about these things and other things pertaining to life. At the end of the day, the father was at home with the whole family having dinner, spending quality time, and teaching the family about God. Remember what **Deuteronomy 6:7** said:

> *"You shall teach them diligently to your children, and shall talk of them when you sit in your house, and when you walk by the way, and when you lie down, and when you rise."* **(ESV)**

The industrial revolution changed things. When fathers took jobs working in the mine, the mill, and factories, it took the father away from the home. When that happened, a lot of the father's responsibilities were left to the mother, and the father's absence was not only noticeable, but felt by the family.

In Paul's letter to the saints at the church of Ephesus, Paul emphasized the fact that part of the father's duties was to teach his children, especially about the things of God.

> *"Fathers, do not exasperate your children; instead, bring them up in the training and instruction of the Lord."* **Ephesians 6:4 (NIV)**

But here we are, over two thousand years later, with a lot of mothers doing the best they can trying to run a single parent home because the father is absent for some reason, not always his fault, but still absent. As we saw earlier when daddy is not around, it affects the mother, the children and the stability of the household.

- It is the **father's responsibility** to be the spiritual leader in the home.
- It is the **father's responsibility** to make known the true and living God to his home.
- It is the **father's responsibility** to educate his household in God's Word.
- It is the **father's responsibility** to be the spiritual warrior of his home.
- It is the **father's responsibility** to lead his household in prayer.
- It is the **father's responsibility** to lead his household to church.
- It is the **father's responsibility** to protect his household both naturally and spiritually.
- It is the **father's responsibility** to pronounce blessings over his children.

When daddy is not around, things that should be enforced are often not, not necessarily because of a lack of effort by the mother, but because, as **Ecclesiastes 4:9** says, *"Two are better than one."* When there's only one trying to manage a household with children, something will inevitably slip through the cracks, and our children are too important for us to let that happen to them.

I don't know if there has ever been a time in history where there is such an urgency for fathers to take the lead in guiding their children to know God, to know His will, to know His ways, and to know His Word.

What do I mean by His will? His desires for us in the time He has given us on this earth. **What do I mean by His ways?** How He functions in line with His divine nature of holiness, righteousness, goodness, kindness, faithfulness, trustworthiness, love, justice, and truth. **What do I mean by His Word?** How He speaks to us through His written word, the Bible, and how it provides for us the knowledge of Him, and the knowledge of how to live a life pleasing to Him.

As fathers, if we lead our children to God, we can make an impact in this world. If we don't, then the killings and tragedies of this world will continue because this generation, who does not know God, His will, His ways, and His word, will *"do what is right in their own eyes"* **(Judges 21:25)**.

- ➤ A generation that does what's right in their own eyes has no problem with taking another person's life.
- ➤ A generation that does what's right in their own eyes has no problem with destroying lives by selling people cocaine, heroin, meth, and drugs laced with fentanyl.
- ➤ A generation that does what's right in their own eyes has no problems kidnapping and grooming young girls and using them in the sex trafficking trade.
- ➤ A generation that does what's right in their own eyes has no problem committing acts of rape, sexual abuse, and sexual acts with children.
- ➤ A generation that does what's right in their own eyes has no problem committing crimes like carjacking, burglary, assault, and

- other felonious crimes.
- A generation that does what's right in their own eyes has no problems promoting acts of racial and religious hatred.

Why are they doing these things? Because without God they are doing what is right in their own eyes and not what's right according to God. Without God in our lives, man has no guardrails to prevent us from falling into evil, wickedness, and the deepest depravity man can find.

A generation that does not know God is a generation without hope.

In recent years, I have spoken to many young people. Often, teenage boys, who are approaching their twenties don't have hope of living past the age of twenty-one.

They believe they will either be the victim of gun violence by some gang, or they will be shot to death by a police officer during a traffic stop, or they will be killed in school, or the mall, or in a movie theater by some mass shooter. **They have no hope.**

Many of them have a different reason for no hope. They live in communities that shout out "No Hope." They live in blighted communities, on streets where most of the homes are either abandoned, boarded up, torn down, or are drug houses. They constantly hear of family members and friends in their community being killed or going to jail. **They have no hope.**

They go to underfunded schools where there are not enough books, or computers, and other teaching aids. They go to schools where teachers are merely babysitters and not concerned with educating them. They go to schools where student fights and gang activity rules the day. **They have no hope.**

And because many of them have no hope, they are overwhelmed with fear, anxiety, worry, and depression. For many, the only way of escape is to use drugs or take their own lives. **They have no hope.**

In their eyes they have no future and no hope. That is why we need fathers to lead their children to God. Hope is found in God. One of the greatest verses in the Bible about hope is found in **Jeremiah 29:11**. It's what God promised His people in those ancient times.

> *"For I know the plans I have for you," declares the LORD, "plans to prosper you and not to harm you, plans to give you hope and a future."* **Jeremiah 29:11 (NIV)**

The hope that God had for His people back then is the same hope that God has for His people today. God wants His people to have a "confident expectation" that they can depend on Him to help them and bring them through their present situation, and to have a prosperous future lined up for them if they just trust and obey Him.

We need fathers to lead their children to God, to pray over their children, and to speak life into their children's existence and future. What do I mean when I say, "Speak Life?" The Bible says, *"death and life are in the power of the tongue"* **(Proverbs 18:21, KJV)**. Instead of discouraging and exasperating our children with negative words, **"words of death,"** we need to encourage them, build them up, inspire them, and affirm them with **"words of life."**

The Father Blessing

In ancient times, fathers would lay hands on their children and pronounce a blessing on them **(Genesis 48:14-16, KJV)**. The blessing would often refer to some positive things the father knew God had in plan for the future of his children. Fathers, we need to pronounce God's blessing over our children that come from the Word of God, and in doing so, believe in God for a **"hope and a future"** for our children.

Fathers, pronounce blessings over your children. Let your children know:

There's greatness within them

There's nothing they cannot accomplish

There are dreams in them that they can make a reality

There are possibilities just waiting for them to bring into being There is no limit on what they can do

They can accomplish anything with God

There are things God has for them they can't even imagine

Fathers, pronounce these things over your children. Speak these things into their lives.

One of my children had difficulties grasping certain fundamentals through elementary school all the way through high school. But this child was also faithful and active when it came to church and serving God and I believed that God would reward this child's faithfulness. One Friday night when my child was in high school, I let them know that God was going to bless their faithfulness and take them beyond their difficulties. Some years later, that same child graduated Magna Cum Laude from a major university in our area. I believe that Friday night, God heard the blessing I pronounced over my child and honored it. God loves to prove Himself.

> **God wants fathers to be the heroes who will lead a generation that does not know Him back to Him.**

~ Journal ~

Chapter 12

"REAL TALK"

As we close, let's take a few moments to have some real talk and real dialogue as we bring things to an end. In the community I grew up in, the men would have real talk in the "Barber Shop." That's where we would come up with all the answers to the world's problems, or so we thought. So, let's have a "Barber Shop" moment and some real talk… Man to Man.

Many men in general have been stigmatized when it comes to being a father because of those men who have abandoned their responsibility as a father. All men are not absent from their children's lives by their own choice.

Some women have unfortunately not allowed fathers to be in the life of their children out of anger and bitterness, using the child as a pawn.

Some women have moved out of state, making it difficult for fathers to have active participation in their children's lives.

Some women have remarried, and to keep peace with their new husband, have decided to limit the interaction the father has with his child.

Whatever the case might be, it may not always be the father's fault why he is not in his child's life like he may want to be, but for those fathers who have willfully decided to not be present in their children's lives, they have made it bad for many other fathers.

And these fathers have given the other fathers a bad name, names that are too often used to put down good fathers who just happen to be in a bad situation. **Here are a few of the names:**

MIA DADS: Missing in Action. Dads who have been missing in their children's lives. These dads are missing when their children need help with their homework. Missing at parent teacher conferences. Missing at their children's important events. Missing at a time of crisis in their children's lives. **MIA DADS**

AWOL DADS: Absent Without Leave. Dads who are biological fathers in name only. Dads who just walked out on their children. Dads who deserted their children. Dads who left their post as fathers to their children. Dads who are visibly and willfully missing in their children's lives. **AWOL DADS**

APB DADS: All Points Bulletin Dads. Dads you must chase down through other people to contact. Dads you can't find when you need them. Dads you can't find in emergencies. Dads who don't respond when you call them or text them. Dads you must put out a family and friends alert to reach them. **APB DADS**

DEAD BEAT DADS: Dads Who Are Dead Beats. Dads who are not willing to put in the work as a father. Dads who don't contribute anything to their children's lives. Dads who don't provide the emotional, spiritual, and financial needs of the child. **DEAD BEAT DADS**

**DESSERT DADS: Dads who are only there for the

Dessert. Dads who are not there for the main course of the child's life. Dads who only show up to reap the benefits of their child's success. Dads who only show up at their child's awards assembly. Dads who only show up at the signing of their child's professional sports contract. Dads who only show up for the photo shoot of their child's achievement and recognition. Dads who are just there for the dessert of their child's life and not the main course of the child's life. **DESSERT DADS**

CONVENIENCE STORE DADS: Dads who are around only when it's convenient for them. Dads who spend time with their children if it doesn't interrupt their plans. Dads who make time for their children when they don't have something else to do. Dads who place convenience over necessity when it comes to the importance of their children. **CONVENIENCE STORE DADS**

Failing to be present and provide for your child goes against the desires of God.

> *"If anyone does not provide for his relatives, and especially for his immediate family, he has denied the faith and is worse than an unbeliever."*
> **1 Timothy 5:8 (NIV)**

Even if you don't live in the same household with your child, you have a responsibility as a father to your child, to provide for and be present in your child's life.

The late writer and director John Singleton's iconic film, ***Boyz n the Hood*** premiered in 1991. The storyline is centered around a teenage boy named Tre and his friends growing up in South Central Los Angeles during the turbulent times of the early 90's when gang violence, drug-dealing, and police abuse of authority was an everyday part of life.

Early in the movie, Tre is being raised by his single mother who has recognized that Tre is at an age (10 years old) when it is critical that his father is actively involved in his life. She meets with his father, and they decide Tre will go to live with him.

Even though the film centers on Tre, I believe the hero of the story is his father. When it came to that pivotal time in Tre's life when he needed the guidance and support of his father in his life, his father did not quibble or make any excuses on why he couldn't do it. He simply rose to the challenge and became the hero his son needed.

"Every man is the hero of his own story"

Recently I heard a phrase, *"Every man is the hero of his own story."* As I researched that phrase, I learned that it meant that a man can rise to the occasion and be the hero of his own story. When it comes to our sons and daughters, and our children in the story of our lives, we as fathers must be that man who is the **"hero of his own story."**

If you haven't been the hero of your own story when it comes to your sons and daughters, and you are ready to become that hero, let me give you a few suggestions on what you should do:

1. Get Gut-Level Honest

Be introspective. Take an honest look at where you are as a father when it comes to your children. God's Word clearly tells us to examine ourselves **(Lamentation 3:40, Galatians 6:4)**. See where you have fallen short of your responsibility as a father. Don't try and make excuses or justify where you have missed the mark as a father but be gut level honest about your failings. It starts with being honest and truthful. Take inventory of yourself as a father. Identify where you could be better as a father, but however you do it, be honest. Ask God to help you be honest.

2. Make Confessions to God

The next thing to do is to confess your failings as a father to God. God already knows, He just wants to make sure you know. He wants you to come to Him and seek forgiveness for where you have missed the mark as a father. God wants you to humble yourself before Him so He can forgive you and lead you through the healing process with your child. Trust me, if you ask God's forgiveness, He will forgive you. *"If we confess our sins, He is faithful and just to forgive us our sins and to cleanse us from all unrighteousness."* **1 John 1:9 (NKJV)**

3. Repent

The word "repent" literally means a "change of heart." It means to turn from one thing to something else. God wants you to have a change of heart when it comes to your responsibility and duty to your child. God wants you to turn from neglecting your child to being "all in" when it comes to your child. God wants to see a 180 degree change in your heart when it comes to being involved in the life of your child. Repentance is a heart matter so ask God to give you a greater desire in your heart to be actively involved in your child's life.

4. Make Amends to Your Children

Just like we must humble ourselves and confess our failings to God, we must humble ourselves before our children and make amends, and that starts by making a sincere confession of our wrongs to them. **James 5:16** says *"Confess your faults one to another."* We must confess to our children how wrong we have been and ask them for their forgiveness. That's just the start. The Bible says, *"faith without works is dead"* **(James 2:26)**. If we are sincere about rebooting our relationship with our sons and daughters, it must be seen in our actions, or all we are really doing is offering empty words and lip service. There must be action in our amends. Investing time with our children, investing money and love in our children, and making up for all we denied them in the past. **James 5:16** continues to say, *"pray one for another."* We need to pray that God will soften our children's hearts so they will receive us into their lives and the relationship will be healed. This is vital because God hears prayer and He responds to sincere prayer that is attempting to accomplish His will, and it's His will that our relations with our children are healed and rebooted.

5. Get Off the Sidelines and Get In the Game

That says it all. Get in your children's game of life and quit sitting on the sidelines. Get invested in their lives, get active in their lives, and let them know that you care about them and love them.

The Greatest Investment

The greatest investment you can make in your child is in their spiritual life. What I'm talking about is pointing them to a right relationship with God through His son Jesus Christ.

This is the greatest thing you can ever do for your child.

- ▶ It's through Jesus Christ that our sins are forgiven.
- ▶ It's through Jesus Christ that we are saved from the wrath of God for our sins.
- ▶ It's through Jesus Christ that we are made right with God.
- ▶ It's through Jesus Christ we are at peace with God and have the peace of God.
- ▶ It's through Jesus Christ we have joy.
- ▶ It's through Jesus Christ that we have eternal life.
- ▶ It's through Jesus Christ that we have God's presence, His Spirit living in us.

➤ It's through Jesus Christ that we have a hope beyond this life.

➤ It's through Jesus Christ we have a home in heaven with God.

Someone once said:

> *"What's the use of bringing your children up in the best neighborhood, sending them to the best schools, so they can attend the best colleges and earn the best grades, and graduate and get the best jobs, to make the best income, to buy the best house, and live in the best exclusive neighborhoods, working to build the best financial portfolios, so they can retire in the best life, only to die and not make it to heaven."*

The greatest investment you can make as a father in your children's life is to lead them to Jesus Christ and pray that they will receive Jesus as their Lord and Savior.

~ Journal ~

~ THE TEN COMMANDMENTS OF FATHERHOOD ~

1. Thou Shalt devote your life to God the Heavenly Father through His Son Jesus Christ.

2. Thou Shalt reverence God the Heavenly Father as an example to your children.

3. Thou Shalt live a godly life before your children.

4. Thou Shalt share the good news of Jesus Christ with your children.

5. Thou Shalt expose your children to the life changing Word of God known as the Bible.

6. Thou Shalt to the best of your ability live at peace with their mother and show her respect.

7. Thou Shalt show your love for your children by giving them your affection, your affirmation, and your attention.

8. Thou Shalt discipline your children when necessary and in a loving and firm manner as instructed by the Word of God.

9. Thou Shalt provide for your children's welfare and needs and always to an encouragement to them.

10. Thou Shalt always pray for your children.

~ THE FATHER COVENANT ~

I enter this covenant with my child and God to be the type of father that treasures them, and I will honor God, the giver of the gift of children. As a father, I will love and cherish my child like my Heavenly Father loves and cherishes me. I promise to give my all as a father, never abandoning my responsibility as their father, and never forsaking my child like my Heavenly Father has never forsaken me. I promise that the child God has entrusted in me will never have to worry about me being absent in their lives, and I will to the best of my ability be a godly example of the type of father God wants me to be.

_____

(Name)

~ ABSENT FATHERS ~
by Rose P. Ratcliffe

Absent fathers still on the run
Working or loafing, thinking it's fun
While mothers toil day and night
Trying to change the wrongs to right
Tis easy to leave your offsprings there
While you gallop and glide, God knows where
Numbers to count, words to be read
Mouths to be fed, little ones to bed
While you're still running, they must be fed

From two people, not one, these children born
Innocent victims of poverty and scorn
Many expect them in life to succeed
While your selfish flight exchange progress to need
Think the scorn and shame kids feel
When dads on the run and naught in the till
When mom must beg, barrow, or steal
Cause the vows he made became unsealed

Are you shocked by laziness, excuses, and fright
Running by day and hiding by night
Are things hanging loose and ends can't meet
Can't you get 'em together?
No, not on the street

Home's the place where families grow
Where parents and children each other know
Where love, joy and play are shared
Where dads finally return, because children cared

Should taxpayers, businesses, welfare, or me
Assume responsibilities while you run free?
Should boys and girls of fathers be deprived
While you run, roam, rip, and hide
Come home dads, cease the false fun
Or you'll soon meet your little ones also on the run
Their paths of rejection, fear, and cold
May chance meet you, "ere the bell tolls"

Footprints, ah! Footprints, many they see
Hoping to find Dad's, he must be free
Free from his roaming and meandering about
Free from the wrinkles of guilt and doubt
Walk straight, stand tall, head for your home
Where children wait, they knew you'd come
You'd cease from running and ponder their fate
And shore mom's commitment before too late

❋ ❋ ❋ ❋ ❋

~ REFERENCES ~

Chapter 1

1. Dr. James Dobson makes the following assertion in his book **"Straight Talk to Men and Their Wives"**

2. *"The Western world stands at a great crossroad in its history. It is my opinion that our very survival as a people will depend upon the presence or absence of masculine leadership in millions of homes."*

Chapter 2

1. *The Fresh Prince of Bel-Air* episode "Papa's Got A Brand New Excuse," directed by Shelly Jensen, aired on May 9, 1994, produced by Werner Walian

2. *Parent's Guide to The Spiritual Mentoring of Teens.* {2} (chapter 6, pg. 84)

Chapter 3

1. National Fatherhood Initiative in Philadelphia, PA, posted on its website in 2022.

2. Author Anthony Campolo, *"It's Friday, But Sunday's Comin'"* (chap 3, pg. 27).

3. Sermon Adrian Rogers "God's Plan for Man the Character of a Real Man."

Chapter 4

1. *Life Application Bible* profile of Absalom.

2. Movie *Gladiator* Director Gridley Scott, produced by Universal Pictures, May 1, 2000.

3. Movie *The General's Daughter*. Director Simon West, produced by Mace Neufeld, Paramount Pictures, June 18, 1999, Writer Nelson Demille.

4. Commentary Gospel of Matthew John McArthur.

5. Henry Blackaby *Encounters with God, Transforming Your Bible Study,* pg. v, foreword).

6. Harry Chapin song, "Cat's In The Cradle," album *Verities & Balderdash*, released October 1, 1974.

Chapter 6

1. Movie *Courageous*. Director Alex Kendrick, Tri-Star productions, released September 30, 2011.
2. Movie *Indiana Jones and the Last Crusade*. Director Stephen Spielberg, Co-writer George Lucas, Paramount Pictures, released May 24, 1989.

Chapter 8

1. Harvard psychologist Samuel Osherson, *Finding our Fathers* — NY: Fawcett/Columbine 1986 (pg.6).
2. Movie *The Wizard of Oz*. Director Victor Fleming, produced by Metro Golden Mayer, released August 25, 1939.

Chapter 9

1. Brya Hanan, Blog "Healing the Father Wound," Hanan Hope & Healing, June 2, 2021.
2. Movie *The General's Daughter*. Director Simon West, produced by Mace Neufeld, Paramount Pictures, June 18, 1999, Writer Nelson Demille.
3. Preacher's Outline and Sermon Bible — Commentary — 2 Samuel, chapter 13 note 6.

Chapter 10

1. Tony Evans, *Tony Evans Book of Illustrations*, pg.103, Moody Press.

Chapter 11

1. Bob Larson, *Extreme Evil: Kids Killing Kids*, Chapter 2, pgs. 30, 31.

Chapter 12

1. Movie *Boyz n the Hood*. Director John Singleton, Producer Steve Nicolaides, Columbia Pictures, released July 12, 1991.

~ ABOUT THE AUTHOR ~

Walter Ratcliffe is retired with nearly 30 years of experience in the criminal justice court system on the municipal, state, and federal level.

He also has over 30 years of ministerial experience, which includes the positions of youth pastor, assistant pastor, and senior pastor.

He is a graduate of Kent State University with a B.A. in Sociology and has studied at Logos Bible College in Akron Ohio, and Temple Bible College in Cleveland Ohio.

He is married and has three adult children.

www.ingramcontent.com/pod-product-compliance
Lightning Source LLC
Chambersburg PA
CBHW051618010526
44119CB00008B/193